LONGMAN CRITICAL E!

C000006839

JULIUS CAESAR

William Shakespeare

Editors:
Linda Cookson
Bryan Loughrey

Longman Critical Essays

Editors: Linda Cookson and Bryan Loughrey

Titles in the series:

CONTENTS

PREFACE

Like all professional groups, literary critics have developed their own specialised language. This is not necessarily a bad thing. Sometimes complex concepts can only be described in a terminology far removed from everyday speech. Academic jargon, however, creates an unnecessary barrier between the critic and the intelligent but less practised reader.

This danger is particularly acute where scholarly books and articles are re-packaged for a student audience. Critical anthologies, for example, often contain extracts from longer studies originally written for specialists. Deprived of their original context, these passages can puzzle and at times mislead. The essays in this volume, however, are all specially commissioned, self-contained works, written with the needs of students firmly in mind.

This is not to say that the contributors — all experienced critics and teachers — have in any way attempted to simplify the complexity of the issues with which they deal. On the contrary, they explore the central problems of the text from a variety of critical perspectives, reaching conclusions which are challenging and at times mutually contradictory.

They try, however, to present their arguments in a direct, accessible language and to work within the limitations of scope and length which students inevitably face. For this reason, essays are generally rather briefer than is the practice; they address quite specific topics; and, in line with examination requirements, they incorporate precise textual detail into the body of the discussion.

They offer, therefore, working examples of the kind of essay-writing skills which students themselves are expected to develop. Their diversity, however, should act as a reminder that in the field of literary studies there is no such thing as a 'model' answer. Good essays are the outcome of a creative engagement with literature, of sensitive, attentive reading and careful thought. We hope that those contained in this volume will encourage students to return to the most important starting point of all, the text itself, with renewed excitement and the determination to explore more fully their own critical responses.

How to use this volume

Obviously enough, you should start by reading the text in question. The one assumption that all the contributors make is that you are already familiar with this. It would be helpful, of course, to have read further — perhaps other works by the same author or by influential contemporaries. But we don't assume that you have yet had the opportunity to do this and any references to historical background or to other works of literature are explained.

You should, perhaps, have a few things to hand. It is always a good idea to keep a copy of the text nearby when reading critical studies. You will almost certainly want to consult it when checking the context of quotations or pausing to consider the validity of the critic's interpretation. You should also try to have access to a good dictionary, and ideally a copy of a dictionary of literary terms as well. The contributors have tried to avoid jargon and to express themselves clearly and directly. But inevitably there will be occasional words or phrases with which you are unfamiliar. Finally, we would encourage you to make notes, summarising not just the argument of each essay but also your own responses to what you have read. So keep a pencil and notebook at the ready.

Suitably equipped, the best thing to do is simply begin with whichever topic most interests you. We have deliberately organised each volume so that the essays may be read in any order. One consequence of this is that, for the sake of clarity and self-containment, there is occasionally a degree of overlap between essays. But at least you are not forced to follow one — fairly arbitrary — reading sequence.

Each essay is followed by brief 'Afterthoughts', designed to highlight points of critical interest. But remember, these are only there to remind you that it is *your* responsibility to question what you read. The essays printed here are not a series of 'model' answers to be slavishly imitated and in no way should they be regarded as anything other than a guide or stimulus for your own thinking. We hope for a critically involved response: 'That was interesting. But if *I* were tackling the topic . . . !'

Read the essays in this spirit and you'll pick up many of the skills of critical composition in the process. We have, however, tried to provide more explicit advice in 'A practical guide to essay writing'. You may find this helpful, but do not imagine it offers any magic formulas. The quality of your essays ultimately depends on the quality of your engagement with literary texts. We hope this volume spurs you on to read these with greater understanding and to explore your responses in greater depth.

A note on the text

All references are to the New Penguin Shakespeare edition of *Julius Caesar*, ed. Norman Sanders.

Michael Gearin-Tosh

Michael Gearin-Tosh is Fellow and Tutor in English Literature at St Catherine's College, Oxford. He is also Associate Director of the Oxford School of Drama.

ESSAY

The opening of *Julius Caesar*

The opening of *Julius Caesar* shows an unusual mirroring of the audience on stage. People have just come together, as we have in the theatre, in order to see a show. In their case it is the triumphal entry of Caesar and the festivity which will follow — some of which we are to see as well. They resent being told to go home, as any audience might:

> MARULLUS   Where is thy leather apron and thy rule?
> What dost thou with thy best apparel on?
>
> (I.1.7–8)

'Rule' is the significant word. The scene is about how the carpenter measures not wood but attitudes and how, as a consequence, he and his friends may be ruled politically.

For twenty lines the cobbler chops logic with the Tribunes, and revels in that playful, punning obstinacy which is an abiding tone among those who, with humour, assert independence in the face of authority. Finally, the cobbler admits that he and his friends 'make holiday to see Caesar, and to rejoice in his triumph' (I.1.30–31). This is the cue for Marullus's long impassioned speech which rules them.

It may be observed that Marullus starts with reasons, but they are to be found only in the first three lines:

> Wherefore rejoice? What conquest brings he home?
> What tributaries follow him to Rome,
> To grace in captive bonds his chariot wheels?

(I.1.32–34)

This comes from Plutarch's *Lives of Noble Grecians and Romanes*, Shakespeare's main source for the Roman plays and one which is followed so closely that Professor Bullough has argued 'it is likely that Shakespeare wrote *Julius Caesar* with North's translation of Plutarch by his side':

> This was the last warre that Caesar made. But the triumphe he made into Rome for the same, did as much offend the Romanes, and more, then any thing that ever he had done before: bicause he had not overcome Captaines that were straungers, not barbarous kinges, but had destroyed the sonnes of the noblest man in Rome, whom fortune had overthrowen.

> *(Life of Julius Caesar)*

'The noblest man in Rome' refers to Pompey, Caesar's great rival, who is the subject of the rest of Marullus's speech.

The distinction between foreign conquest and civil war is one which Marullus might have developed. Plutarch dwelt on it at some length: Rome has been weakened by the loss of a family which produced great leaders; Caesar appears to have acknowledged the distastefulness and impropriety of a triumph for civil war victories by not requesting it before:

> And bicause he had plucked up his race by the rootes, men did not thinke it meete for him to triumphe so, for the calamities of his contrie, rejoycing at a thing for which he had but one excuse to alleage in his defence, unto the gods and men: that he was compelled to doe that he did. And the rather they thought it not meete, bicause he had never before sent letters nor messengers unto the common wealth at Rome for any victorie that he had ever wonne in all the civill warres: but did alwayes for shame refuse the glorie of it.

> *(Life of Julius Casesar)*

There were further arguments which lie behind the events

of the play and were known to Shakespeare and the educated part of his contemporaries. Pompey has advanced the cause of the common people against the Senate, yet had retained its respect. He had restored the legal guardians of the people, the Tribunes — and it is two Tribunes, Flavius and Marullus, who plead for his memory in this scene. Caesar, in contrast, had already violated the constitution of Rome — most famously, he had crossed the Rubicon. Pompey was notably averse to the plunder and rapine practised by successful Roman generals: Caesar, burdened by debts, was much less so. Pompey's domestic life has been called 'pure and simple', Caesar's was irregular and the subject of scandal.

The appeal of Pompey was such that the historical Brutus supported him against Julius Caesar, despite the fact that Pompey had executed Brutus's own father. Shakespeare would have read this in Plutarch:

> Afterwards when the Empire of Rome was devided into factions, and that Caesar and Pompey both were in armes one against the other, and that all the Empire of Rome was in garboyle and uprore: it was thought then that Brutus woulde take parte with Caesar, bicause Pompey not long before had put his father unto death. But Brutus preferring the respect of his contrie and common wealth, before private affection, and perswading himselfe that Pompey had juster cause to enter into armes then Caesar: he then tooke parte with Pompey, though oftentimes meting him before, he thought scorne to speake to him, thinking it a great sinne and offence in him, to speake to the murtherer of his father.

> *(Life of Brutus)*

All these factors could have given Marullus ample material if he had chosen to give reasons why 'the respect of his contrie and common wealth' or Pompey's 'juster cause' should lead the cobbler and his friends to withdraw their support from Caesar. However, the substance of Marullus's speech is a description:

> You blocks, you stones, you worse than senseless things!
> O you hard hearts, you cruel men of Rome,
> Knew you not Pompey? Many a time and oft
> Have you climbed up to walls and battlements,

> To towers and windows, yea, to chimney-tops,
> Your infants in your arms, and there have sat
> The livelong day, with patient expectation,
> To see great Pompey pass the streets of Rome
>
> (I.1.35–42)

Instead of argument, there is visual dislocation. The world looks different from 'walls and battlements', even more different from 'towers' and you may be dizzy clinging to 'chimney-tops' — 'yea' seems to suggest that they are even higher than towers, at least more precarious, and perhaps both. People who are perched so high have a new perspective in which normal life is dwarfed and wider horizons seem to be their natural element. This heady rapture, too, is not momentary. It lasts 'the livelong day', the length seems to make it a form of life, the mix of exhilaration and 'patient expectation' has time to establish itself. Nor is the height lonely — infants are 'in your arms' and there is the warmth and passion of a crowd waiting excitedly.

At last, the climax occurs:

> And when you saw his chariot but appear,
> Have you not made an universal shout,
> That Tiber trembled underneath her banks
> To hear the replication of your sounds
> Made in her concave shores?
>
> (I.1.43–47)

The formula has echoes in the 1930s and '40s: a crowd leaves ordinary life behind to wait for a leader, and when *il Duce* or the *Führer* appears there is such acclaim that the essential power of the universe seems to reside in this mystic union of prince and people. Tiber is not an ordinary river god. The River Tiber is the river of Rome and tutelary deities were worshipped by the Romans, especially those of their own sacred city which governed the world. To make Tiber tremble is, in this sense, to put a god in subjection to the very people he has fostered. Even Tiber's masculinity is overthrown — commentators have been struck, as T S Dorsch notes in the Arden edition by *her* banks: 'the feminine possessive adjective sounds strange when applied to the Tiber ... regarded by the Romans as essentially masculine.'

Marullus stuns the crowd into submission by his picture.

His next lines are rebukes delivered with overt and formal rhetoric:

> And do you now put on your best attire?
> And do you now cull out a holiday?
> And do you now strew flowers in his way,
> That comes in triumph over Pompey's blood?
> Be gone!
>
> (I.1.48–52)

It is unusual to find two incomplete lines so close to each other in such a moment as lines 47 and 52. They are a mark of utter confidence in the victory which is later articulated by Flavius:

> See where their basest mettle be not moved:
> They vanish tongue-tied in their guiltiness.
>
> (I.1.61–62)

In his moment of victory Marullus went so far as to speak like a holy prophet:

> Run to your houses, fall upon your knees,
> Pray to the gods to intermit the plague
> That needs must light on this ingratitude.
>
> (I.1.53–55)

When the common people leave, Flavius urges him:

> Disrobe the images,
> If you do find them deck'd with ceremonies.
>
> (I.1.64–65)

Marullus hesitates:

> May we do so?
> You know it is the feast of Lupercal.
>
> (I.1.66–67)

This was one of the most important and ancient religious rites of Rome, probably pre-Roman in origin. Held in February its purpose was to purify the land and secure its fertility and prosperity in the coming year. The Romans were superstitious about procedure. There is, therefore, much cause for surprise in Flavius's reply, 'It is no matter'. We must conclude that religion is one thing when ruling the poor but quite another when it comes to the actions and attitudes of rulers themselves.

All good openings establish an idiom, intimate themes and create imaginative space. In *Julius Caesar*, however, Shakespeare goes a step further. He enacts one of the major sources of dramatic tension in the play. People are subjected to a piece of oratory. We discover what moves them. And because they to some extent mirror us, we are alerted to our own vulnerabilities in the hands of a fiery speaker. As Swift observed, man is not a rational animal, only one which is capable of reason. Orators know how to dislocate that capacity, and the first scene enacts in little the explosion of *Julius Caesar* in Act III.

The benefit of such anticipation is that it enriches our later response. When Cassius urges in Act II scene 1 that Antony be killed, the argument is that Antony is an able plotter:

> I think it is not meet,
> Mark Antony, so well beloved of Caesar,
> Should outlive Caesar. We shall find of him
> A shrewd contriver; and you know his means,
> If he improve them, may well stretch so far
> As to annoy us all; which to prevent,
> Let Antony and Caesar fall together.
>
> (II.1.155–161)

His 'means' could refer to his wealth or, more likely, his connections. The topic of oratory is raised neither by Cassius nor by any of the Senators present, and our general impression of Antony in this scene comes from Brutus:

> Alas, good Cassius, do not think of him.
> If he love Caesar, all that he can do
> Is to himself: take thought, and die for Caesar;
> And that were much he should; for he is given
> To sports, to wildness, and much company.
>
> (II.1.185–189)

'Much company', in the measured voice of Brutus, means too much company or too addicted to company: Antony is a man so sociable, good humoured and over-festive that he lacks character and he will not take an independent line on a serious issue — 'And that were much he should', he would never go so far. This is not a man who will have developed the concentration and detached watchfulness of the orator:

> TREBONIUS There is no fear in him; let him not die;
> For he will live, and laugh at this hereafter.
>
> (II.1.190–191)

We learn otherwise on Antony's entry after the assassination. Brutus speaks as flat a line as can easily be imagined:

> But here comes Antony. Welcome, Mark Antony.
>
> (III.1.147)

Antony ignores Brutus's welcome. Indeed he negates it with a farewell:

> O mighty Caesar! dost thou lie so low?
> Are all thy conquests, glories, triumphs, spoils
> Shrunk to this little measure? Fare thee well.
>
> (III.1.148–150)

This is the utterance of a natural orator, fluent, passionate and demonstrating. Marullus's visual dislocations in the first scene are more than equalled by Antony's sense of different scales in the shrinking of so much grandeur to the mere extent of a corpse.

Whether or not we consciously recall Marullus's oratory at this point, the first scene has given us a feeling for what orators can do in its enacting of their power. This is enough to generate terror when Antony makes his request:

> That's all I seek,
> And am moreover suitor that I may
> Produce his body to the market-place,
> And in the pulpit, as becomes a friend,
> Speak in the order of his funeral.
>
> (III.1.226–230)

We now suspect what seems so casual. And we sense that Brutus's view of Antony is complacently patronising. When a man of Antony's ease has depths, his liking for 'wildness' may make him dangerously creative, and his fondness for 'much company' may give him a popular touch. This is a formidable combination. There are few more lethal weapons in politics.

AFTERTHOUGHTS

1

Do you agree with Gearin-Tosh's opening comments regarding the significance of the word 'rule' (page 9)?

2

Explain the relevance to Gearin-Tosh's argument of the references to Plutarch at the beginning of this essay (pages 10–11).

3

Do you agree with the Arden editor that the references to the Tiber as feminine sound 'strange' (page 12)?

4

What parallels does Gearin-Tosh suggest between the effectiveness of Marullus's oratory in the first scene and the later events of the play?

Ian Haywood

Ian Haywood lectures in English at Roehampton Institute, and is the author of numerous critical works.

ESSAY

'A savage spectacle': reproducing Caesar

The assassination of Julius Caesar on the steps of the Capitol in Rome is one of history's most dramatic events. Many other Roman rulers met similar fates, but Caesar's death has exerted a particularly powerful hold on the imagination. Remember the way he is killed: he is stabbed by some of his closest supporters and friends, notably Brutus. He is betrayed on the threshold of the building which symbolises his power (the British equivalent today might be the Houses of Parliament). He is killed in public. We respond to these details so strongly because we imagine them to be some of the deepest insecurities of tyrants: a sudden, exposed, humiliating overthrow. Put another way, the event satisfies our own deep misgivings about tyrannical power. Unless such crucial emotions about the nature of society were involved it is unlikely the ides of March would have achieved such mythical status. Myths and legends are ways in which cultures tell stories about themselves in pleasurable forms in order to try to resolve very deep tensions and uncertainties. This 'deep structure' is like the mind's unconscious which contains the repressed, antisocial desires of infancy (the most celebrated of these is of course the Oedipus complex). Although these desires have been 'locked away', they are constantly attempting to break through into our conscious life and therefore need regulating. Freud believed dreams served this function, but myths and literature were also ways in which the repressed could 'return' in socially acceptable forms. A story can be endlessly recycled, endlessly experienced, endlessly reproduced. In reading or seeing *Julius Caesar* we can experience unconsciously our desire as a society to rebel against arbitrary authority, the political equivalent of a parent figure. Freud extended and modified the Aristotelian notion of catharsis, whereby drama (particularly tragedy) purges the audience of painful emotions. Politically this conclusion is conservative. I hope to show the meanings of *Julius Caesar* are in fact as radical as the central event.

In his analysis of dreams, Freud drew a distinction between the dream itself and its underlying meaning. The 'manifest' content is the subject matter we recall, and the 'latent' content is the unconscious significance. We are able to reach the deeper understanding by careful scrutiny of the signifying processes of the dream (Freud called this the 'dreamwork'). The most important of these is symbolism, the means by which objects are given latent, often sexual meaning. Freud's model is useful to us in three ways. Firstly, it prevents us confusing representation and meaning. The significance of a ritual or symbol must be decoded — this is an active procedure. The action of *Julius Caesar* will give us clues to its meanings, but its power (like Caesar's) must be rigorously demystified. Secondly, as already hinted at, dreamwork is analogous to literary criticism, the attempt to discover or uncover the ways the text exerts influence over us. Thirdly, the emphasis on symbols seems particularly appropriate for a play which foregrounds the social ritualisation of political power. The focus on the cultural reproduction of Caesar is an additional factor in the play's appeal: it is a play about the myths of power. The play's 'manifest' content is actually 'dreamwork'. The conspiracy led by Brutus and Cassius is primarily an assault on the myth of Caesar which sustains and legitimates his position. We must be careful not to identify too closely with the conspiracy, however. Although they are radical decoders of Caesar's myth, they are still part of the text's manifest content, and its own mythical power.

Political control works by securing consent as well as threatening force. The former is aimed at the mind, the latter at the body. It is preferable for those being ruled to at least appear to be willing or happy subjects, even if they have never been provided with the intellectual or material means to make a truly free choice. To secure consent will involve the political manipulation of the major institutions of personal development (family, education), communication (media) and those public activities and spaces where people traditionally feel less constrained: entertainment, leisure and collective rituals. Much of the action of *Julius Caesar* takes place in this public urban space. The outdoor locations (street, forecourt of government buildings, market-place) are arenas where society's orderly compliance can be visibly manifested. Large numbers of people are allowed to gather and circulate, but they must not try to control the space or its cultural meanings. That would signify a state of political unrest and instability, as is the case at the opening of the play, though Shakespeare introduces a clever twist.

It appears at first as if the upholders of authority and the law are the Tribunes Marullus and Flavius. They rebuke the festive workers for being on the streets on a normal working day but not wearing their workclothes: the 'sign /Of your profession' (I.1.4–5). This is an interesting offence to begin the action of the play. The crowd are infringing the dress code which exists to enforce class distinctions. An artisan must look like an artisan, or else the social order which depends on the regulation of 'signs' is destabilised. The Tribunes are outraged by the display which signifies both a voluntary rejection of work ('you idle creatures ... Is this a holiday?' (I.1.1–2)) and a challenge to the visual control of class identity. Marullus and Flavius are desperate to reclassify the crowd through language: 'what trade art thou?' (I.1.5) precedes the demand for an explanation. Language, like dress, is a system of signs that orders and controls the way we perceive the world. The control of language is essential for maintaining authority. The radical potential of the crowd is enhanced by their playful refusal to give the Tribunes a straight answer. The punning and witty indirection allows them to dictate the pace of the exchange and resist the imperative language fired at them. This is the verbal equivalent of their sartorial challenge to social classification. It is a carnivalesque use of language; extrovert, creative, crossing boundaries, irreverent, non-referential, mischievous (the Tribunes use 'saucy' and 'naughty' — like parents scolding insolent children). At the height of this display, however, there are two startling surprises. We discover (like the Tribunes) that the explanation for the crowd's activity is that they are there to celebrate the return of Caesar to Rome. In other words the event is lawful and a public ritual designed to bolster, not threaten, the power of the state. The second surprise (in Aristotle's terms a 'reversal') is that the role of subversive is then taken over by the Tribunes. They are still outraged and bullying, but now for completely unexpected reasons.

Marullus asserts linguistic control of the situation by attacking Caesar's reputation and guilt-tripping the crowd. He accuses them of betraying their previous loyalty to Pompey (the implication being that Pompey was also betrayed by his one-time ally Caesar), of being insincere and transferring their emotional loyalties easily from one leader to the next. Of course Marullus's aim is exactly such a transfer of loyalty, but in the reverse direction. In order to achieve this he uses the first example in the play of oratory: heightened, extravagant, melodramatic language designed to win over an audience to a political argument. Oratory is the dramatic discourse of government, and contrasts sharply with the carnivalesque language of the 'senseless' crowd. The harangue re-inscribes the social distinctions between speaker and audience while overtly denying the authority of Caesar. Marullus wants a new ruler but not a new social order. He is an arch-imperialist: his first criticism of Caesar is to call into doubt his military prowess ('What tributaries follow him to Rome,/ To grace in captive bonds his chariot wheels?', I.1.33–34). Freeing Rome from Caesar's 'bondage' is seen through the legitimate bondage of others. More important, perhaps, is the substance of Marullus's speech, which is a description of one of Pompey's triumphant homecomings. The intention is to shame the citizens who are now about to cheer Caesar's victory over Pompey. Marullus rivals the present spectacle with one of his own. He tells a story, and the effectiveness of the speech relies on the power of the story. He invests Pompey with larger-than-life significance while simultaneously divesting Caesar of it. His speech shows the importance of stories for the reputation of rulers. The production of mythic power requires the constant reproduction of fictions and icons sustaining that power. Marullus demonstrates that cultural reproduction is also the area where the political struggles are fought, and meanings contested. Notice that Flavius and Marullus leave the stage to 'disrobe the images' of Caesar. This act will cost them their lives, but its true significance is to emphasise the iconoclastic nature of their rebellion. Vandalising the ceremonially bedecked statues is to refuse the Caesar myth — the essential step to take before vandalising his body. (How odd that the Tribunes did not realise the crowds wère celebrating two great public events: Caesar's homecoming and the feast of Lupercal. One explanation for this astonishing lapse is that without it the latent challenge to the 'signs' of social order in the confrontation with the crowd would not have been as effective.)

A statue is usually an ideal image of an important person. Its function is to celebrate and commemorate that individual, and its prominent position in public spaces signifies a superior status. The mythic importance of an individual can often be gauged by the frequency of the images in various forms. The profile of a ruler is often stamped on coins and printed on banknotes. Although these are not works of art, they are given the same iconic function as a statue or bust. One of the hall-marks of political power is its privileged ability to circulate throughout society images of itself.

It is no surprise therefore to see statues featuring promi-nently in *Julius Caesar*. We have already noted the disrobing of the Lupercal statues by the Tribunes. The next striking recur-rence is Calphurnia's prophetic dream, which depicts a statue of Caesar spouting blood (II.2.76–79). We may wonder why it is a statue and not Caesar himself bleeding, given that the latent content of the dream seems so obviously to be a warning of an assassination attempt. The answer should now be apparent: the dream signifies the puncturing of Caesar's image. The half-human, half 'senseless' characteristics of a bleeding statue collapse the distinction between the man and the myth, and show their dependency on one another. That is precisely how Cassius operates upon Brutus. Cassius does not present a cata-logue of Caesar's corrupt or tyrannical deeds, but like Marullus produces fictions to show that Caesar the imperfect human being is not worthy of the colossal myth emanating from that body. One might say that Marullus attacks the image and Cassius the man. Cassius 'disrobes' Caesar metaphorically by exposing his physical failings (interestingly enough in the swimming of the Tiber escapade neither Cassius nor Caesar strips, but Caesar's performance clearly suffers). We shall return to this metaphor later, but it is worth pointing out that the play seems to share Cassius's intention of dramatically displaying Caesar's infirmities. The absurdity of accruing god-like status on a mortal is apparent to the spectator inside and outside the play.

Caesar is persuaded by Decius to ignore the ominous dream (II.2.83–90). Decius wins the contest to secure the most favourable interpretation of the dream's symbolism. He controls the meaning of Caesar's image, and effects a striking political change. That formula is repeated in the play: Marullus to the craftsmen; Cassius to Brutus; Mark Antony to the crowd.

One of Antony's ploys in his speech to the assembled crowd is to reconstruct the assassination. In his account, Caesar fell 'at the base of Pompey's statue,/ Which all the while ran blood' (III.2.189–190). Antony's imagination may have added the supernatural detail. His speech is very gory, although there was a legend that the body of a murdered man would bleed in the presence of its murderer. The detail is both poignant and dramatic. It reminds us of Calphurnia's dream, and reinforces the parallel between the two rulers first drawn by Marullus. But more importantly we see that Antony makes far more use of Pompey's statue than the conspirators. His account reproduces the bleeding statue to dramatic effect. The conspirators missed a golden opportunity to seize a powerful symbol that lay right at their fingertips and display its new meanings. Unfortunately they were too interested in trying immediately to mythify their deed: firstly through a gory ritual, and secondly by speculating on future theatrical representations of the event (III.1.111–113). It may seem indulgent for Shakespeare to introduce a reference to the theatre at this juncture in the play, but for that reason the intrusion is particularly important. The point is not that Brutus and Cassius are prophesying their future fame, but that they see theatre as a political practice. Each time Caesar 'bleeds in sport' the meanings of the 'lofty scene' will be contested in the present. The reference also drives home the intimacy of theatre and politics. Although bathing their swords and arms in Caesar's blood is a very dramatic (and risky) quasi-religious ritual, designed to both visually shock and reassure the spectator, Mark Antony has a much sharper sense of the theatricality of politics. His famous speech, as we shall see shortly, combines brilliantly the techniques of iconoclasm and mythification.

Caesar himself is not in full control of his image. When he is first onstage his mortal imperfections are foregrounded: superstition, physical infirmity (strikingly contrasted with the stripped Antony). His conscious efforts to enhance his divine status through stage-managed public spectacle happen offstage and are reported to us. Of course the reported scene would be difficult to enact on stage (not, incidentally, on film — cinema's myth-making qualities have always been its main appeal). But the dramaturgy does confirm the division between Caesar and his image. I have made this point several times and in some ways it seems common sense: we all know there is a difference between a role and the person who holds it. But myths of power often rely on blurring this distinction, achieving a mystification of both the role and the person, and mingling politics and personality. A more spurious distinction between the public and the private is often laid on top of the role–holder dichotomy. The private realm is supposed to be shielded from the public world, and the 'free' human being can speak. In fact *Julius Caesar* shows quite the opposite. The parallel scenes involving Caesar and Brutus in their domestic situations are deeply permeated by political language and action. Though he is in his most 'private' space, Caesar cannot disentangle himself from his myth ('Caesar shall forth', II.2.10), which effectively paralyses him. He cannot see that the role is more important than he is, precisely because the myth relies on reproducing idealised images of himself. He seems to believe the myth and become subservient to it, which is one factor in his downfall. Notice that his most idealistic self-presentation is at the very point he is about to be stabbed. His image will not protect him, despite its statuesque qualities ('prayers would move me;/...I am constant...', 'Unshaked of motion', III.1.59–60, 70). On the contrary, the conspirators believe that only by puncturing the body can the myth be deflated. This may also be a mistaken belief, but Brutus becomes convinced that divesting of power requires assassination. His word for myth or image is 'spirit', and he sums up the dilemma and the dichotomy thus:

> We all stand up against the spirit of Caesar,
> And in the spirit of men there is no blood.
> O, that we then could come by Caesar's spirit,
> And not dismember Caesar! But, alas,
> Caesar must bleed for it.

(II.1.167–171)

The resolution is not entirely satisfactory either in terms of language or subsequent action. The weakness of the argument is shown when Brutus continues with the speech. He relies heavily on metaphor, as was the case in his famous garden soliliquy (II.1.10–34). A metaphor works in a similar way to myth by transferring properties from one object to another. In comparing Caesar in the garden soliloquy to a ladder climber, serpent's egg, and sacrificial dish, Brutus was fighting for control over the meanings of Caesar, but only now is he doing so to serve the ends of assassination. The metaphor is convincing rhetorically (at the level of myth) but not analytically. Enough of Caesar's 'spirit' is left intact for Mark Antony to resurrect it. Caesar can then become a literal spirit (a ghost) to rub the point in (and even then it is the assassination that haunts Cassius and Brutus: the event which released this particular meaning of 'spirit').

Before we move on to Antony's manipulation of the crowd, one further motif needs commenting on. We touched on it when we discussed the intention of the Tribunes to 'disrobe the images'. We then followed up the significance of statues, but we could equally have followed up the examples of disrobing: Antony stripped for the Lupercal race; Caesar spuriously bearing his breast to the crowd; further breast-bearing of the conspirators to the prodigious storm, Antony to the conspirators, and Cassius to Brutus. The most striking instance is of course Antony's unveiling of Caesar's corpse. All these moments have differing 'local' meanings, but it would not be fanciful to claim that taken together they show the play's interest in the vesting and divesting of power. Brutus, we remember, is appalled that the conspirators come to his house at night covering their faces

(II.1.77–79). His real disgust, however, is at the need for secrecy, and as soon as Caesar is dead Brutus's desire for openness and exposure (besmearing the swords, allowing Antony to speak) leads him astray. Rule by consent will try to present itself as open, accountable, even vulnerable when necessary (hence the various breast-bearings). The polarities are secret–exposed and covered–hidden. For a myth to function it needs to be circulated and exposed though it may be about very secretive things.

Finally, then, to Antony's speech (III.2.74–108). It has a legendary status all of its own, for Antony is able to convert a crowd of newly-won Brutus supporters into a riotous mob. Their anarchic violence is the demonic echo of the festive crowd at the beginning of the play — both switch political allegiance, both are used as political tools. The 'commons', as they were known in Shakespeare's time, have an ambivalent status. Their consent is sought after, but they are manipulated into granting it, and despised for being so malleable. The conspirators judge their ability to see through the Caesar myth against the unthinking acceptance of the lower orders. But though Brutus acts for the good of 'the general', they remain an abstraction to him: a remote ideal. Mark Antony understands them far better. In modern terminology his approach is determinedly 'tabloid'. He uses the tactics of emotive language, dramatic display and material reward to reconstruct Caesar's image. His most masterful touch, of course, is having secured Caesar's body. This enables him to reinvest the body with mythic significance, but also to turn the iconoclastic tactic of divesting (disrobing) to his own ends. The religious connotations of the body have been present throughout the play. It is appropriate to treat the body of a 'divine' ruler like that of a martyred saint. But we must be wary of accepting this version of Caesar. Antony exploits the body as much as the crowd. He is the greatest fictionaliser of the play. He promised he would make Caesar's wounds speak through him, and he achieves this in lavish detail. The conspirators could not have known Caesar would 'bleed in sport' so soon. Antony animates the body (an echo here of the bleeding statue motif). He covers it in language, and exposes it physically. His rupturing of conventional sign-systems releases the antisocial energies of the crowd, in a mockery of insurrection. We know Antony has Octavius and Lepidus waiting to bring help. Antony could have gone to join them. His success in the market-place was not guaranteed. The lack of a credible motive gives the scene even more power. We see the cynical reality of the reproduction of Caesar exposed by its greatest practitioner.

That is not the end of the story. We have not glimpsed the 'true' Caesar. The struggle for control of Caesar's image is reproduced with each new interpretation of the play. We may all need myths of power, but we must continue to contest their meanings.

AFTERTHOUGHTS

1

Explain the importance to Haywood's argument of his opening references to the theories of Freud (pages 17–18).

2

Do you agree that 'The control of language is essential for maintaining authority' (page 19)?

3

How do you explain the Tribunes' apparent ignorance of what the people are celebrating (page 21)?

4

What significance does Haywood attach in this essay to statues?

John E Cunningham

John E Cunningham currently divides his time between writing and travel. He is the author of numerous critical studies.

ESSAY

Elements so mixed

'The play should really be called *The Tragedy of Brutus.*' Discuss and illustrate with close reference to the text.

Generations of examinees and young essayists have been asked to address themselves to this topic. They have duly noted Brutus's agony in the orchard (where he says that he knows of no personal cause to move against Caesar, only that of the public good); his love of his worthy wife; the fact that he would not let his fellow-plotters kill anyone other than Caesar; the tottering support of Caius Ligarius who rises from his bed when he hears Brutus is involved in the conspiracy; and Brutus's careful oration to the plebeians, as well as his austere refusal to:

>   wring
> From the hard hands of peasants their vile trash
> By any indirection

(IV.3.73–75)

Such essays usually end by quoting the tribute paid to him — by an enemy, no less! — 'This was the noblest Roman of them all' (V.5.68).

Commentators at a more academic level enjoy pointing out how Shakespeare got it wrong: that Caesar did not speak his last words in Latin, but said, in Greek, 'And you, my son' —

perhaps glancing at the Roman tale that he and Brutus were indeed father and son, though this is of interest only in that it supposes an extraordinary degree of enterprise in Caesar at the age of fourteen. And of course Brutus divorced his first wife merely because he wanted to marry Portia, a widow with three children; he later gave himself the presumptuous title of *imperator*; he and Cassius did not die on the same day; and his introspective soliloquies are chiefly of interest as a possible exploration of what would be done in this way so much better in *Hamlet*.

We may begin our own assessment at the end. Antony's obituary speech — which he can afford to make when he has successfully hounded its subject to his death — does not provide the last words of the play. These are given to Caesar's nephew and adopted son Octavius, who is already emerging as the clear-headed realist who will oust completely the too easy-going Antony and become himself the first emperor, as Julius Caesar almost certainly would have done had he not been killed. Octavius says of Brutus:

> According to his virtue let us use him,
> With all respect and rites of burial.
> Within my tent his bones tonight shall lie,
> Most like a soldier, ordered honourably.

> (V.5.76–79)

and then he turns briskly to the business of the day and of the future. Let Brutus, he says, be treated as he deserves — and he emphasises the word 'virtue', which Shakespeare would know was a very Roman concept. In Latin it implied not only moral strength but physical toughness and courage, being linked with the ordinary word for a man (*vir*), which survives in English in 'virile'. Roman *virtus* implied a number of things beyond that — a certain austerity, for example, which imposed on all adult males a very simple garment of white wool, a fidelity to the supposed civil integrity which, long before the events of this play, had driven out the despotic Tarquin kings and established the republic, its principles now threatened by Caesar with another tyranny. So there is even a political slant to virtue here, as well as the highly practical one of being prepared to serve the country in time of war — and Octavius would have his body treated 'most like a soldier'. The Elizabethans too valued personal courage and seem to have been highly patriotic in the face of the enemy — Catholic Spain for example — but they were not anything like republican in their political sentiments: fifty years after this play was written, even Cromwell had to crush the too-egalitarian Levellers. The Elizabethans valued a stable succession — which was beginning to look distinctly dodgy when this play was first performed — and from this viewpoint Caesar's last words have a special interest:

> But I am constant as the northern star,
> Of whose true-fixed and resting quality
> There is no fellow in the firmament.

(III.1.60–63)

This is often held to be dramatic irony, for the audience knows that in a moment this fixed star will fall; however he does not fall — not in spirit — but lives on to haunt the battlefield and defeat the conspirators; his successor takes up the role of unifier of the empire to which he had aspired and, as it turned out, Augustus (Octavius's title when he became Rome's first emperor) was a 'constant' ruler. It can hardly escape the modern reader or spectator that when Caesar is cut down after this lofty speech, the assassins — they are no less — shout 'Liberty! Freedom!' and so on with all the meaningless fervour that has been shown by a thousand trigger-happy liberation armies since, before a terrified populace. The Elizabethans distrusted and abhorred revolution as deeply as some Marxists were to come to believe in it, and there can be no doubt that they felt the noble Brutus really had to go: a decent man, give him a respectable funeral — in short, they agreed with Octavius.

But, we are reminded, it is Antony's elegy that is so memorable — that has been quoted out of context as often as his plea for ears in the market-place, by people who have never read or seen the play. Let us move one step back, from Octavius's to Antony's tribute. He discusses not only Brutus's motives — which turn out to have been 'honourable', the word he had so effectively turned into a sneer in the market-place — but his character too: 'the elements/ So mixed in him'. What does this mean?

One 'element', in our sense of that ambiguous word, we have

already detected: Roman virtue. To Shakespeare the universe was made up of four elements — earth, air, fire and water — complementary to the four humours of the human microcosm, blood, choler, black bile and phlegm, which determined, by their proportions, the general types of which we all belong: sanguine, choleric, melancholy and phlegmatic. Cassius speaks of 'that rash humour which my mother gave me' (IV.3.119) and earlier in the same scene Brutus asks him:

> Must I stand and crouch
> Under your testy humour?
>
> (IV.3.45–46)

This humour is easily identified: Cassius is a choleric man, that is, one whose emotions, particularly anger, are quickly aroused and take control of him. Cassius is indeed an angry man, outraged that any other human being should be able to look down on him, as he says in the great scene in which he introduces Brutus to the idea of revolt: his 'lean and hungry look' bespeaks a sort of perpetual frustration. His friend, by contrast, is highly controlled, his emotion always restrained: even when he is suffering great private grief at the news of his wife's death, he does not lose his temper with Cassius, sternly as he rebukes him.

Brutus, then, seems to be phlegmatic, a type which interested Shakespeare, partly perhaps because it was a challenge — it is not easy to make very restrained people dramatically exciting — partly it may be because he found something to envy in this quality. When Hamlet addresses his phlegmatic friend Horatio, in a classic reference to the subject, he says:

> and blest are those
> Whose blood and judgement are so well commeddled
> That they are not a pipe for Fortune's finger
> To sound what stop she please. Give me that man
> That is not passion's slave . . .
>
> (III.2.78–82)

If person's character was made up of a mixture — a 'complexion' — of the humours, then we may also see in Brutus a rather more subtle shading than in Horatio. Brutus shows some signs of introspection, a quality that would be associated with melancholy: certainly there is something sad in his essentially lonely figure. Thus in the scene in the orchard (II.1), after a few exchanges with Lucius, he embarks on a soliloquy in which he examines his own motives for doing something untypical of a man of judgement — political assassination. A little later, reading the paper that Lucius found under the window, he muses a little on his own ancestry, famous for helping to drive out the Tarquin kings. And, where Cassius dies cursing himself for living 'To see my best friend ta'en before my face' (V.3.35), Brutus ends with a statement of his own feelings:

> Night hangs upon mine eyes; my bones would rest,
> That have but laboured to attain this hour.

> (V.5.41–42)

In this last, melancholy utterance we can see another 'element' that has been strongly developed throughout the play: the rather bleak notion that our life is simply a process of dying is typical of a kind of stoicism, and philosophically Brutus is a Stoic, another contrast with his friend Cassius, who 'held Epicurus strong' (V.1.76).

Stoicism, superficially unattractive to many today, was popular in Renaissance Europe for several reasons. It was materialistic in that it taught the universe was purely physical, an attractive idea to those who were turning away from the more superstitious aspects of medieval religion; it offered a code of conduct based on reason — and thus self-control — which appealed to the awakening intelligence and awareness of the times; it taught that all men are brothers, a notion which endears itself to any age of liberal tendencies. A later age still — in this country the nineteenth century — was to select one ingredient for special emphasis: the patient endurance of physical or mental pain — the stiff upper lip syndrome. In this sense of the word today we describe someone as 'stoical'.

This quality indeed Brutus displays, most notably in the quarrel in the tent with Cassius, when he is suffering bereavement himself. Portia shows a corresponding courage in the first of her brief scenes:

> Tell me your counsels, I will not disclose 'em.
> I have made strong proof of my constancy,

> Giving myself a voluntary wound
> Here, in the thigh; can I bear that with patience,
> And not my husband's secrets?

(II.1.298–302)

Brutus later explains the mental discipline which he has used to fortify himself against the time when this remarkable partner should die:

> With meditating that she must die once.
> I have the patience to endure it now.

(IV.3.189–190)

This then is the 'philosophy' which Cassius unwittingly accused him of forgetting when he gave way to 'accidental evils'. Yet there is something repellent about a system of thought which regards our life simply as something to be endured as well as possible. The original Stoics were interested in life's possible purposes, but the brand of stoicism that Shakespeare best knew had been filtered through the Roman dramatist Seneca, whose violent and bloody plays, intended for reading rather than performance, had been rediscovered, translated, adapted and imitated, not least by Shakespeare himself in *Titus Andronicus*, one of the most rarely acted of his works. The view of life that Seneca leaves with us is nihilistic, however, and Shakespeare is one of the great life-asserters: at the end of his direct tragedies the business of life is always resumed; and his comedies — Brutus never laughs, though he can smile at Lucius's weakness for sleep — are immensely positive.

The subject of our hypothetical examination question now seems, for all his courage and integrity, to be a somewhat negative being. Those addicted to the theory of the 'tragic flaw' adapted by later critics from a suggestion of Aristotle, will say that here we have a true tragic hero, whose 'flaw' is his own honesty. Yet a careful examination suggests that what is wrong with Brutus is that he is unable to understand what other people in general are like — he thinks that they are all like him, an assumption as stupid as it is implicitly arrogant; and though, as we shall see, he has learned some rhetoric, one of the three arts that every educated member of Shakespeare's audience would have studied, along with the grammar of classical languages and logic, his ability in the last of the three subjects turns out to be feeble indeed.

By the time we are permitted to share his thinking, in the scene in the orchard, we already know what Cassius feels about him:

> Well, Brutus, thou art noble; yet I see
> Thy honourable metal may be wrought
> From that it is disposed: therefore it is meet
> That noble minds keep ever with their likes;
> For who so firm that cannot be seduced?

(I.2.305–309)

And indeed Brutus is ready to be seduced by feigned eloquence and forged letters, never dreaming that his friend could stoop to such tricks. His own mind is made up by the time he opens his first soliloquy with the blunt 'It must be by his death' (II.1.10). By what reasoning has this most reasonable of philosophers arrived at this fearsome conclusion? By a series of general propositions about human nature and the effects of success and power on ambitious men. By what facts are these propositions supported? By the meaningless statement 'Everybody knows' ("tis a common proof') and by a series of metaphors, about ladders and serpents' eggs. Aristotle, who reasoned in a more real apprehension of the world than Brutus, prohibited the use of figures of speech in logic as being inherently fallacious; it is a fallacy to which Brutus repeatedly turns. When the conspirators raise the question of whether they should kill anyone besides Caesar, and Cassius speaks of the danger to them if Antony lives, Brutus dismisses this suggestion — thus, effectively, ruining their entire action and killing the lot of them — again basing his case on a series of images, culminating in 'Let us be sacrificers, but not butchers, Caius' (II.1.166). The distinction may be clear to him, but would hardly be so to Caesar who, with his 'three and thirty wounds' seems indeed to have been as nearly butchered as makes no difference.

That this trick of false reasoning is no accident of dramatic verse is surely borne out when we look at the last, fatal decision that Brutus makes — again in the face of Cassius's sensible opposition. Brutus says they must press on to Philippi, when his friends want the enemy to waste their strength in marching to meet them. The clinching speech is often quoted:

> There is a tide in the affairs of men,
> Which, taken at the flood, leads on to fortune;
> Omitted, all the voyage of their life
> Is bound in shallows and in miseries.

(IV.3.216–219)

This persuasive metaphor is, quite simply, untrue: the commonest proverb — 'He that fights and runs away lives to fight another day' for example — denies it. It sometimes *seems* with hindsight to be true, the basis of many an 'If only . . .' fantasy, but is no basis at all for the exigencies of military strategy. Here it is disastrous.

But then Brutus does not really understand the 'men' of whose affairs he speaks so knowingly. We said earlier that he had learned some oratory. It is often said that Antony's speech to the crowd is a masterpiece of this art; it is less often noted that Brutus's preceding oration is that of someone who had been well schooled in public speaking. There is a careful sequence of conditions and consequences:

> Romans, countrymen, and lovers, hear me for my cause, and be silent, that you may hear . . . Censure me in your wisdom, and awaken your senses, that you may the better judge.

(III.2.13–17)

There is also balanced alliteration here, even a sort of pun (censure–senses). Later there is one of those cumulative sentences with a dramatic finish beloved of classical orators:

> As Caesar loved me, I weep for him; as he was fortunate, I rejoice at it; as he was valiant, I honour him; but, as he was ambitous, I slew him.

(III.2.24–26)

This, together with a whole series of 'rhetorical' questions, suggests that he has certainly done his homework. What he fails wholly to grasp is that, when addressing a crowd quite unlearned in the arts of oratory, they will not really be listening to reasons, however carefully these are presented, but hankering for facile emotion. Antony is certainly 'no orator, as Brutus is' (III.2.218), as he ironically says; he is a superb rabble-rouser, one who knows how to play on instinctual things like greed and a mob's ever-ready disposition to violence, one who can throw them a slogan to shout in derision — the 'honourable man' taunt — who can use objects like the torn cloak and the will, with which he plays peek-a-boo, rather than objective reasoning, to dangle before the Roman thickheads who had followed Brutus's careful argument so ill that one of them had cheerfully shouted 'Let *him* be Caesar!' after he had spoken. Such a mob responds to a demagogue, and that is the role that Antony, quite cynically, plays. When he has them roaring for blood, he disclaims whatever 'mischief' they may perpetrate: their first action — significantly, the only one we are shown — is to kill an innocent insomniac. These are the 'brothers' of the Stoics' view of man.

Yet there is a worse irony to come. Cassius kills himself in a simple error, which arises for no more reason than that he is literally myopic and must rely on another man's faulty view of the course of the battle. Brutus dies in the error of judgement in which he has lived with such awesome steadfastness:

> My heart doth joy that yet in all my life
> I found no man but he was true to me.
> I shall have glory by this losing day
> More than Octavius and Mark Antony
> By this vile conquest shall attain unto.

(V.5.34–38)

Which is eloquent, deeply touching — and wrong. Cassius is false to him from the beginning, working quite deliberately upon the 'noble metal' of his friend by persuasion, even by forgery, exploiting his name relentlessly to lend a cover of respectability to his own bloody, personal enterprise. Antony, who shook his hand and promised fidelity, was planning even as he did so to use his very honour as a source of slander and innuendo, and to pursue him to his death. Brutus dies, as he lived, failing to comprehend what most of us are actually like: a disastrous man to hold power, one might think, compared with the young Octavius, already showing himself a realistic master of situations and men.

As to the glory of the losing day: Antony is famous still, not least for his powers or persuasion as shown in this play, even more as a half of one of the greatest of all love-stories; Octavius went on to become the first Augustus, ruler over Rome's most distinguished period, remembered in our summer calendar two thousand years later. Brutus has such immortality as may be conferred by a thousand examination essays; but at least Shakespeare lets him die happily ignorant of how things really are. This may be pathos, but it is not tragedy.

AFTERTHOUGHTS

1

Explain the relevance to this essay of Cunningham's analysis of the theory of the humours (pages 30–32).

2

How admirable do you find Brutus's stoicism (pages 32–33)?

3

Do you agree that 'Brutus dies in the error of judgement in which he has lived' (page 36)?

4

Compare the concluding sentence of this essay with that of the essay by Campbell (pages 79–89). With which, if either, do you agree — and why?

Neil Taylor

*Neil Taylor is Dean of Arts and
Humanities at Roehampton Institute. He
is the author of numerous critical works.*

ESSAY

Reading in *Julius Caesar*

When Shakespeare's Julius Caesar tries to read the character of
Cassius his first observation is that 'He reads much' (I.2.200).
Shakespeare also characterises Brutus as a reader (probably
following Plutarch, who wrote of Brutus that, during the campaign against Caesar, he 'did nothing but study all day long').
He is reading the stars when we meet him in his private
orchard; when he thinks of going indoors his destination is his
study (II.1.2–3, 7). At Sardis he carries a book in the pocket of
his nightgown (IV.3.250–251).

Reading is a central device in the play. The very first scene
establishes the topic. It begins with Flavius trying to persuade a
crowd of workmen that they have misread the calendar:

> Hence! home, you idle creatures, get you home:
> Is this a holiday? What, know you not,
> Being mechanical, you ought not walk
> Upon a labouring day without the sign
> Of your profession?

> (I.1.1–5)

Flavius is now trying to 'read' the clothes and utensils which
signify the workmen's trades. If we allow the term 'reading' to
mean the act of interpreting the signs in *any* sign-system, not

just the sign-system of written language, then the play yields up a whole range of 'readings'.

In the next scene, for example, the crowd is involved again. This time, however, their signs are offstage — inarticulate, ambiguous shouts and flourishes. Brutus hazards an unguarded reading:

> I do fear the people
> Choose Caesar for their king.

> (I.2.79–80)

A few lines later, Caesar and his retinue come on stage and Brutus asks Cassius to help him read their faces:

> But look you, Cassius,
> The angry spot doth glow on Caesar's brow,
> And all the rest look like a chidden train:
> Calphurnia's cheek is pale, and Cicero
> Looks with such ... fiery eyes.

> (I.2.181–185)

Soon, Casca is co-opted as a reader of signs, describing for Brutus and Cassius (and us) the offstage spectacle of Caesar's theatrical rejection of the crown. He alone is our source for the information that Antony offered Caesar the crown, that Caesar 'foamed at the mouth, and was speechless', that Cicero spoke in Greek, and that the tag-rag people treated Caesar and Antony like 'players in the theatre' (I.2.258). In this scene we therefore read Brutus reading Casca's reading of Antony and Caesar's play without the play.

The Act closes with Cicero and Cassius joining Casca as readers — this time of a system of supernatural signs, 'prodigies' and 'portentous things' (I.3.28, 31). The point is made that signs can sometimes be read wrongly:

> ... men may construe things after their fashion,
> Clean from the purpose of the things themselves.

> (I.3.34–35)

In Act II, Brutus becomes not only the focus of a political plot but identified for us as a man who reads in error. He is taken in by the bogus letters planted for him to read. When his wife brings him her wounded thigh to read, he is preoccupied with his own problems and misreads her distress as being less significant than it proves ultimately to be (she later kills herself out of anxiety on his behalf). Brutus merely promises to read for her later the 'charactery' of his brows, i.e. what is written in the lines of his furrowed forehead (II.1.308). Meanwhile, in Caesar's house, they are reading entrails and dreams, and disagreeing in their readings.

In Plutarch, Caesar's assassination is very brutal:

> Caesar turned him no where but he was stricken at by some, and still had naked swords in his face, and was hacked and mangled among them, as a very beast taken of hunters. For it was agreed among them that every man should give him a wound, because all their parts should be in this murther: and then Brutus himself gave him one wound about his privities.
>
> *(Life of Caesar)*

> Brutus caught a blow on his hand . . . and all the rest also were every man of them bloodied.
>
> *(Life of Brutus)*

At first sight, Shakespeare seems to have ignored much of his reading of Plutarch's accounts. His only stage direction is the laconic *'They stab Caesar'*. Nevertheless, Shakespeare introduces the imagery of the hunt in Antony's later (imagined) version of the killing: 'Julius! Here wast thou bayed, brave hart;/ Here didst thou fall; and here thy hunters stand' (III.1.204–205). And in the next line Antony begins to read the visual imagery with which he is confronted.

He points to the blood clinging to the conspirators. He goes on to describe them as being crimsoned in Caesar's lethe, and *signed* in his spoil (III.1.206). Earlier, Brutus has called upon the conspirators to sign themselves in quite a different language:

> Stoop, Romans, stoop,
> And let us bathe our hands in Caesar's blood
> Up to the elbows, and besmear our swords;
> Then walk we forth, even to the market-place,
> And waving our red weapons o'er our heads,
> Let's all cry, 'Peace, freedom, and liberty!'
>
> (III.1.105–110)

How is the red to be read? Brutus is aware that Caesar's blood is ambiguous and therefore exhorts his fellow-conspirators: 'Let us be sacrificers, but not butchers' (II.1.166). But who is to say what range of readings operates when Antony grips the conspirators' 'purpled hands' (III.1.158) in ritual order?

> First, Marcus Brutus, will I shake with you;
> Next, Caius Cassius, do I take your hand;
> Now, Decius Brutus, yours; now yours, Metellus;
> Yours, Cinna; and, my valiant Casca, yours;
> Through last, not least in love, yours, good Trebonius.
>
> (III.1.185–189)

The theatrical paint accumulates on Antony's hand. Does it spell his cunning, his hypocrisy, his kinship with Caesar, or his kinship with the conspirators? His care for life or his carelessness with the lives that are to be shed? It is a multiple pun, valid in all its readings. Ambiguity at its most creative.

A scene later Antony gives a public reading. not just of Caesar's will but of Caesar's body too:

> Look, in this place ran Cassius' dagger through;
> See what a rent the envious Casca made
>
> (III.2.175–176)

Antony is brilliant in his uses of ambiguity ('For Brutus is an honourable man'), but he chooses to use it for ultimately destructive ends:

> Now let it work. Mischief, thou art afoot,
> Take thou what course thou wilt.
>
> (III.2.262–263)

The Act ends with further ambiguity and a tragic case of misreading. The illiterate Plebeians tear Cinna the poet for his verse, as a poet might tear up his verses, but they do so because they fail to distinguish between two bearers of the same name. How many similar clerical errors occur as a result of Antony pricking names in the first line of the following Act?

In Act IV Brutus and Cassius quarrel. Cassius is driven to imagine that all his faults have been observed by Brutus, then:

> Set in a notebook, learned, and conn'd by rote
>
> (IV.3.97)

Cassius, the great observer who looks quite through the deeds of men (I.2.201–202), suddenly wonders if he has lost the ability to read Brutus:

> I did not think you could have been so angry
>
> (IV.3.142)

But his major error was his original reading of Brutus. He failed to read enough of Brutus's nature to foresee his behaviour beyond the decision to kill Caesar. That failure overshadows Cassius's early success in reading Brutus's ability to convince himself of the necessity to assassinate his friend.

The battles of Act V bring with them flags, ensigns, signals, portents, bills — all demanding readings. Cassius dies because he relies on Pindarus to describe and to interpret yet another offstage spectacle, the supposed capture of Titinius. Titinius protests to the short-sighted, but now dead and therefore deaf, Cassius 'Didst thou not hear their shouts?/ Alas, thou hast misconstrued every thing!' (V.3.83–84).

Thus far it has been the characters within the play who have been doing the reading and misreading. But Shakespeare has written the play in such a way that it raises the question of its own readability. Its presentation of characters and events is essentially ambiguous and resistant to stable readings.

For example, G Wilson Knight found two Caesars in Caesar:

> He is two incompatibles, shifting, interchanging. As the hour of his death draws near, this induces almost a sickening feeling, like a ship's rocking. This is the uncertainty, the unreal phantasma of Brutus' mind . . .
>
> (*The Imperial Theme*, 1931)

We cannot tell from Caesar's words and behaviour how accurate is Brutus's fear that he might accept the crown which Antony offers him. There is no way of knowing whether Brutus's reading, the reading which Cassius can read in Brutus, is a misreading. Shakespeare deliberately refuses us that privilege.

This ambiguity is, in an intellectual sense, the starting point of the play. At the dramatic conclusion of the play there is ambiguity too, but of quite another kind. Act V ends with Antony's reading of Brutus as 'the noblest Roman of them all' and Octavius's reading of Philippi as 'this happy day' (V.5.68,

81). *Was* Brutus noble? Is Antony sincere? Is this day, on which Brutus dies, happy? Shakespeare will not answer these questions.

Other ambiguities are less clearly intentional. Just as the Plebeians are confused by the two Cinnas, E M Forster points out the presence of two Cascas:

> Casca at first appears as extremely polite and indeed servile to Caesar. 'Peace, ho! Caesar speaks,' he cries. Then he shows himself to Brutus and Cassius as a sour blunt contradictious fellow, who snaps them up when they speak and is grumpy when they invite him to supper. You may say this is subtlety on Shakespeare's part, and that he is indicating that Casca is a dark horse. I don't think so. I don't think Shakespeare was bothering about Casca.
>
> *(Two Cheers for Democracy*, 1951)

Then there is Portia, who undergoes two 'deaths'. This last case brings to light a division in Brutus. When Brutus first hears of Portia's death he confesses to being sick of many griefs (IV.3.142). When, presumably by some error on Shakespeare's part or on the part of his transcriber, he hears the news for the second time, he bears the truth stoically, like a Roman (IV.3.186). In one case Brutus is moved, in the other unmoved.

Brutus feels himself to be the heir to the philosophy of political liberty embodied in his ancestor, Lucius Junius Brutus, who 'did from the streets of Rome/ The Tarquin drive, when he was called a king' (II.1.53–54). But he also feels himself to be the heir to the philosophy embodied in his father-in-law, Marcus Porcius Cato, the Stoic. Stoicism is the Roman ideal of constancy, the condition of being unmoved and imperious, but utterly loyal to self, friends, Rome and one's ideals. At the news of Portia's death Cassius urges Brutus to make use of Stoic philosophy and in the quarrel scene Brutus determines to follow 'that philosophy/ By which I did blame Cato for the death/ Which he did give himself' (V.1.100–102). What this means is that Brutus intends to kill himself, as Cato and other Stoics had.

However, Brutus complicates the matter:

> I know not how,
> But I do find it cowardly and vile,

> For fear of what might fall, so to *prevent*
> The time of life . . .

(V.1.102–105, my italics)

Ah! says Cassius:

> Then, if we lose this battle,
> You are contented to be led in triumph
> Thorough the streets of Rome?

(lines 107–108)

But Brutus replies:

> No, Cassius, no; think not, thou noble Roman,
> That ever Brutus will go bound to Rome;
> He bears too great a mind.

(lines 110–112)

Is Brutus committed to patient endurance or to suicide? We are as confused as is Cassius.

There is a moment at Philippi when there appears to be more than one Brutus on the battlefield. Antony reads the situation correctly and proclaims of one of them:

> This is not Brutus . . .

(V.4.26)

At other times in the play it is not so easy to define identity. Some of our multiple readings of a character like Brutus may be attributable to Shakespeare's exploration of the moral conflict which Brutus lives through. Some of them may arise from Shakespeare's exploration of the split between the private and the public figures Brutus is obliged as a Senator to be. Some of them may arise from Shakespeare's interest in the exploration of psychological conflict. Some of them may arise merely from slackness in Shakespeare's writing. Some of them, finally, may arise from the fact that Brutus and his assassination of Caesar are public property. Shakespeare cannot ultimately control our readings of such famous figures and incidents.

There are moments in many of his plays when he momentarily acknowledges that he is writing a play. *Julius Caesar* has its own moment when the play comes close to reading itself. This moment is the assassination of Caesar in the Capitol. While

Caesar turns a deaf ear to his suitors' verbal entreaties, his assassins translate their desires into the language of deeds:

CASCA Speak hands for me!
CAESAR *Et tu, Brute*? — Then fall Caesar!

(III.1.76–77)

Some speeches call attention to their own language in a way that demands that they be read as being especially significant. The personal significances for Brutus and for Caesar of the act of betrayal implicit in the assassination are foregrounded through the words *'Et tu, Brute'*. But Caesar's sudden switching into Latin has a curious, multiple effect. Shakespeare read about the assassination in Plutarch's *Lives of the Noble Grecians and Romans*. In the *Life of Caesar* there is an account of how Casca struck Caesar in the back of the neck with his sword. Then both men cried out:

> Caesar in Latin: 'O vile traitor Casca, what doest thou?" and Casca, in Greek, to his brother: 'Brother, help me'.

Plutarch wrote in Greek. Shakespeare read him in Sir Thomas North's 1579 English translation (of a French translation of a Latin translation of the Greek). It was Shakespeare's idea to have Caesar switch into Latin when he addresses Brutus.

The effect is to focus attention on Brutus. But the artifice of the unprecedented transition from one language to another also calls attention to itself. And, being Latin, *Et tu, Brute* sounds (quite spuriously) like a quotation from the real Julius Caesar. In combination with the self-dramatisation of 'Then fall Caesar!', it suggests not only a historical significance but one which Caesar himself somehow comprehends.

Thus, in suppressing the Greek-speaking Casca but addressing his substitute in Latin, Shakespeare reorganises the structure of the action and, at the same time, gives prominence to language. Furthermore, there is the suggestion that Caesar has access to a special language, a sign-system operating beyond the play itself and providing discourse for those who read the Literature of History and the History of Literature.

AFTERTHOUGHTS

1

How is the term 'reading' being applied in this essay?

2

Do you agree that Caesar's blood becomes a 'multiple pun, valid in all its readings' (page 42)?

3

How do you react to the ambiguities highlighted by Taylor on pages 44–45?

4

Do you agree with Taylor's analysis of the effect of the Latin '*Et tu, Brute*' (page 46)?

Cedric Watts

Cedric Watts is Professor of English at Sussex University, and the author of many scholarly publications.

ESSAY

Julius Caesar, III.1.111–113

This essay is about layered ironies: conceptual and political ironies. The title refers to the following speech by Cassius:

> Stoop then, and wash. How many ages hence
> Shall this our lofty scene be acted over,
> In states unborn, and accents yet unknown!

The context of the speech is worth recalling. The conspirators have assassinated Caesar, who has displayed courage and dignity in his death (*'Et tu, Brute?* — Then fall Caesar!'). Some moments of confusion follow: a mixture of elation, tension, uncertainty and improvised planning. Then, in response to Casca's remark that an early death saves one from years of apprehension, Brutus says:

> Grant that, and then is death a benefit:
> So are we Caesar's friends, that have abridged
> His time of fearing death. Stoop, Romans, stoop,
> And let us bathe our hands in Caesar's blood
> Up to the elbows, and besmear our swords;
> Then walk we forth, even to the market-place,
> And waving our red weapons o'er our heads,
> Let's all cry, 'Peace, freedom, and liberty!'

> (III.1.103–110)

Here Cassius makes his exclamation about the 'lofty scene', and Brutus caps it by exclaiming:

> How many times shall Caesar bleed in sport,
> That now on Pompey's basis lies along,
> No worthier than the dust!

(III.1.114–116)

In this essay, I intend to consider the implications of Cassius's words, for they are peculiarly resonant and richly ironic.

1

'Stoop then, and wash', says Cassius. He endorses Brutus's plan to ritualise the murder. By deliberately smearing themselves in blood, the conspirators symbolise their readiness to share responsibility for the assassination and to declare publicly their commitment. A rather messy killing is here being tidied by ritual and rhetoric. This symbolic ceremony was devised by Shakespeare; Plutarch's *Lives*, his main source, says only that the assassins became smeared with blood in the general mêlée, in which some of them accidentally wounded each other. Shakespeare confers on the historic event the conspirators' attempt to dignify it by ritual. In turn, however, the context mocks their attempt ironically. In the theatre, their excited rhetoric is mocked by the stillness of Caesar's corpse, which lies beside them; and the smearing of their swords and arms ('Up to the elbows') in blood resembles an unholy sacrament or profane baptism, an open acknowledgement of murderous guilt which challenges their idealistic words. The proposed cry, 'Peace, freedom, and liberty!', inevitably seems ironic when uttered by men who flaunt the blood of a ruler whose 'freedom and liberty' have been so belligerently curtailed.

Consider again the resonance of the words:

> How many ages hence
> Shall this our lofty scene be acted over,
> In states unborn, and accents yet unknown!

In the first place, the words are strikingly self-validating. A historic event, the actual killing of Julius Caesar in ancient Rome, is being re-enacted; re-enacted (in Shakespeare's day) in Elizabethan England, a state 'unborn' in Caesar's time, and proclaimed in 'accents yet unknown' — Elizabethan English, not classical Latin. The fictional killers are making a speculative prophecy which is automatically fulfilled by the very fact of the play's performance. In modern times, the prophecy is even more emphatically fulfilled, since the states in which stage productions are seen may include those 'unborn' (from the colonisers' if not the indigenes' viewpoint) in Shakespeare's day: Canada or Australia, for instance; and the 'accents yet unknown' may include American accents or, if the play is being performed abroad in translation, German or Russian or Japanese. The prophecy, then, was not only curiously self-validating in the Elizabethan period; it has gained ever greater validation as Shakespeare's works have travelled on through time and round the world. When Cassius refers to 'this our lofty scene' which shall be 'acted over', he uses explicitly theatrical imagery; the fact of political murder is being likened to a noble piece of theatre which will be given a continuing historic immortality in stage productions. This meaning is emphasised by Brutus's concurrence: 'How many times shall Caesar bleed in sport' — bleed stage-blood, for entertainment.

One critic, Catherine Belsey, has suggested that if Shakespeare's plays make explicit references to fictionality, this valuably destroys the theatrical illusion. It is as if the play then says to us: 'Don't be fooled by me. Let me remind you that I'm only a lot of words by Shakespeare, not reality at all.' In the case of *The Winter's Tale*, she says that when a character compares the fictional action to a story, this 'has the effect of undermining the illusion'.[1] Belsey believes that readers of stories are so naïve that they are constantly in danger of mistaking the story for reality, and therefore it is ideologically desirable that a text should prick the bubble of illusion by declaring itself to be merely discourse. (Perhaps Belsey should remind the readers that her own critical account is merely discourse, and that we

---

[1] Catherine Belsey, *Critical Practice* (London and New York, 1980), p. 101.

would be naïve victims of illusionism were we to imagine that we were reading words uttered by Catherine Belsey which relate directly to realities.) If we test her theory against Cassius's words, we may well find that the text operates in ways more complicated than her rather schematic approach suggests.

When Cassius speaks of 'our lofty scene', he is speaking metaphorically about the events within the fictional world of which he is a part. If we are in the audience and the play is working reasonably well, so that our disbelief is sufficiently suspended, consistency within that fictional realm will be maintained. When, however, he invokes those future times in which the assassination will be enacted as fiction in theatre, it is likely that alertly responsive members of the audience will at once see the irony that what is before us is indeed a re-enactment of the kind prophesied; and the effect will become retrospective as the prophecy itself is then identified as part of the theatrical enactment. A conceptual paradox thus occurs. It is as though the imaginary Rome briefly dissolves to reveal the performance as *contemporary* performance; even though, as the scene proceeds, the imaginary Rome once more gains priority in our imaginations. Belsey's notion that spectators tend to be readily fooled into confusing representation with reality still imputes too great a credulity to theatre audiences. If we were really fooled, then no doubt some of us would have rushed on stage to attempt to save Caesar or, if we were persuaded by the conspirators' arguments, to deliver some thumps and kicks to his collapsing body. In the eighteenth century, Samuel Johnson came close to the truth when he declared:

> It will be asked, how the drama moves [us], if it is not credited. It is credited with all the credit due to a drama. It is credited, whenever it moves, as a just picture of a real original ... The delight of tragedy proceeds from our consciousness of fiction; if we thought murders and treasons real, they would please no more.
>
> Imitations produce pain or pleasure, not because they are mistaken for realities, but because they bring realities to mind.[2]

---

[2] *Johnson on Shakespeare*, ed. Walter Raleigh (London, 1908), p. 28.

In the case of *Julius Caesar*, the claim that 'they bring realities to mind' has double force, because we know that Caesar was a historical person and that his assassination really took place; so a very specific reality is invoked as well as the less specific realities (the likely behaviour of a ruler under attack, the likely response of the murderers) that are part of our imaginative field of reference.

2

The phrase 'lofty scene' has multiple ironies. Indeed, the assassination of a ruler as powerful as Caesar is the stuff of great tragedies, as Cassius knows. But his phrase is part of a deliberate, conscious attempt to vindicate murder by endowing it with noble significance. Audiences have just seen one man — an ageing, partly deaf man — being ambushed, goaded, and finally stabbed to death by numerous conspirators. It looks like a messy, nasty death; and, quite probably, our imaginative sympathies are extended to Caesar, the outnumbered but plucky underdog in the situation, while our imaginative antipathy is likely to be directed against the assassins. When Brutus offers the feeble argument that the conspirators have actually done their victim a favour by 'abridg[ing]/ His time of fearing death' (III.1.104–105), we may smile sceptically at this rationalisation of treacherous murder. Furthermore, though the action is 'lofty' in the sense that it has historical importance, it is not necessarily 'lofty' in the sense of having noble dignity; again, we sense the endeavour by the conspirators to vindicate their action retrospectively. They seek to convert gory deed into glamorous story. Certainly Caesar will, as Brutus foretold, 'die in sport' on many occasions. Polonius offers confirmation when he remarks to Hamlet, 'I did enact Julius Caesar. I was killed i'th'Capitol. Brutus killed me' (III.2.112–113), and Polonius will, ironically, be assassinated himself soon after making this remark. The large irony unrecognised by Brutus and Cassius is that when their action is re-enacted in the theatre, they may well be seen at that point as villains, or, at best, as naïvely misguided political activists, rather than as heroes. Of course, responses will vary, as will the actors' and directors' interpretations; but it is hard to acclaim the killers of an unarmed victim, and the dead Caesar's silence is at least as eloquent as Cassius's rhetoric.

Whenever the scene is performed, says Cassius:

> So often shall the knot of us be called
> The men that gave their country liberty.

(III.1.117–118)

What the play shows, of course, is that far from inaugurating an era of liberty, the conspirators inaugurate an era of bloody conflict: Brutus and Cassius are obliged to go into battle, and are defeated by the alliance of Mark Antony, Octavius and Lepidus (and by their own misjudgements). Audiences readily sympathise with underdogs, and Brutus and Cassius become more sympathetic as they face defeat. We know from *Antony and Cleopatra* that the victorious triumvirate will in turn fall to dissension, and eventually Antony will die defeated by the ruthless and calculating Octavius. Even before the end of *Julius Caesar*, there are portents of this dissension to come: in IV.1.18–28, Antony persuades Octavius to conspire with him against Lepidus; and at V.1.16–20, Octavius insists on overruling Antony's tactical judgement. So, politically, the paraphrasable message of *Julius Caesar* seems much the same as that of *Hamlet* or *Macbeth*. It is the following, apparently conservative, message. People who conspire to depose or kill the rightful ruler may succeed for a while, but they may be burdened with guilt, they will provoke increasing disorder, and they themselves may well be defeated and killed in turn. Brutus and Cassius die defeated; Claudius will be slain; so will Macbeth. One Tudor political orthodoxy (repeated by Gaunt in *Richard II*, I.2.37–41) was that only God should judge and condemn a ruler; subjects should submit, even if that ruler was corrupt. A crucial exception to this maxim was that rebellion against a usurper might be justified. We have good evidence that in Shakespeare's day, as now, plays could be interpreted politically in most variable ways. The Earl of Essex's supporters paid Shakespeare's company for a special performance of *Richard II* on the eve of Essex's rebellion against Queen Elizabeth. (Evidence that this was the play by Shakespeare, and not someone else's *Richard II*, is that the deposition episode — IV.1.154–317 — was omitted from every text of his play printed during Elizabeth's reign.) Although that is the drama in which the conservative orthodoxy is made explicit by Gaunt, as well as by the Bishop of Carlisle and (of course) Richard himself, what presumably mattered to the rebels was the simple fact that the work depicted a successful rebellion against a lawful monarch. It seems, therefore, quite likely that when *Julius Caesar* was originally performed, some spectators would have been inclined to select from the play's many possibilities a subversive message commending republicanism, even though others might well have derived a message harmonious with their loyalist inclinations. (Caesar's ghost arrives to make an ominous prophecy to Brutus, and the prophecy is fulfilled, so the plot's metaphysic is ranged in opposition to the assassins.) Since the play was offered as entertainment dramatising hypothetical possibilities, many spectators might well have taken all its political matter with the large pinch of salt that we sprinkle on the ideological notions of any such entertainment. Shakespeare was a sophisticated dramatist and not a messenger-boy.

3

There remains a final dimension of irony to Cassius's exclamation, 'How many ages hence/ Shall this our lofty scene be acted over . . .!' Brutus takes the words to mean that in the future, the assassination of Caesar will be performed on stage. There is, of course, another meaning, of which Cassius may be unaware. The theatrical metaphor can be allowed to remain simply metaphor instead of being converted into a literal prediction of fictional drama. If the metaphor remains unconverted, then what is being predicted is that in the historical future, not on stage but in bitter reality, political assassinations will take place: Brutus and Cassius will have provided precedent for subsequent bloody deeds, undertaken perhaps in the name of 'Peace, freedom, and liberty', which, like their own misconceived venture, will result not in a new Golden Age but in further bloodshed, fresh disillusionment, and the restoration of Caesarism — of autocracy in one form or another. Modern audiences may recall that the English Civil War, in which Charles I was executed, resulted in the autocratic 'Protectorate' of Oliver Cromwell. They may recall that the French Revolution, with its watchwords of *'Liberté, Egalité, Fraternité'*, resulted in the carnage of the guillotine, the invasion of republican Switzerland by the revolutionary army, and eventually in the emergence of Napoleon as autocratic emperor. Or they may recall that the communistic ideals of the Russian revolutionaries were mocked by the subsequent triumph of Josef Stalin. For us today, therefore, there is a peculiarly grim irony in the sanguine hopes of Brutus and Cassius that their deeds will be re-enacted 'in states unborn, and accents yet unknown'. Shakespeare's bloodstained conspirators have indeed proven to be truer prophets than they (or even their author, perhaps) could ever have foreseen.

AFTERTHOUGHTS

1

Do you agree that Caesar 'displayed courage and dignity in his death' (page 48)?

2

Explain the significance of the 'conceptual paradox' identified by Watts on page 51.

3

How 'conservative' (page 53) or 'subversive' (page 54) do you find *Julius Caesar*? Do you think it matters how a play is received by its audience?

4

What further examples occur to you in support of Watts's closing remark that the conspirators have 'proven to be truer prophets than they... could ever have foreseen' (page 55)?

Peter Thomson

Peter Thomson is Professor of Drama at Exeter University, and the author of numerous critical works.

ESSAY

The significance of decisions in *Julius Caesar*

However Cassius may have fascinated students of 'character' in the work of Shakespeare, it is the opposition of Caesar and Brutus that dominates the action of *Julius Caesar*, and that domination persists even after the death of Caesar. We do well to remember that the structure of the play has not always been admired. The Duke of Buckingham was speaking for the orderly eighteenth century, which considered Shakespeare remarkable but unruly, when he refashioned *Julius Caesar* into two plays, the first preserving Shakespeare's title, but the second named after its hero, *Marcus Brutus*. We do well also to remember that, when he wrote the play, Shakespeare was entering knowingly into a Renaissance controversy over the assassination of Caesar.

Some writers chose to portray the assassins as enemies of the ideal state. The most famous example is in Dante's *Inferno*, where Brutus and Cassius share the lowest circle of Hell with Judas Iscariot. Others, like Montaigne, condemned the historical Julius Caesar, viewing his murder as the proper punishment for tyranny or pride. Shakespeare, we may agree, is not conclusively of either party. Like Plutarch, from whom he derived his plot and (by way of North's magnificent translation) a high proportion of his language, he succeeds in establishing a political situation too volatile and dangerous to allow the independent play of either morality or heroism any kind of unqualified approval. That is not to say that Shakespeare considered morality and heroism to be less important than political intelligence, but it is to suggest his awareness that, in matters of state, neither morality nor heroism can usefully operate in isolation from political intelligence. The 'old' view that Shakespeare was some-how 'above' politics cannot long survive an alert reading of *Julius Caesar*. He understood well enough the extent to which politics is the art of making decisions, and I shall be arguing that, in *Julius Caesar*, he draws our attention to the art of decision-making (or the fatal artlessness of decision-making) with the utmost deliberation.

It seems to me quite clear that the crucial decisions of Caesar and Brutus are closely observed and emphatically under-lined in the text. Furthermore, the context in which they are to be made is carefully prepared:

> Here is a mourning Rome, a dangerous Rome,
> No Rome of safety for Octavius yet.

> (III.1.288–289)

These words of Antony's, spoken after Caesar's assassination, might with equal appropriateness be spoken at the beginning of the play, after the death of Pompey. The first three Acts are heavy with an almost claustrophobic sense of danger, which culminates in the tearing apart of Cinna the poet, reminiscent for Elizabethan audiences of the 'quartering' of traitors after they had been hanged and drawn. The linguistic insistence on the dangerous state of Rome is begun in the first scene, and carried through to its final lines from Flavius:

> These growing feathers plucked from Caesar's wing
> Will make him fly an ordinary pitch,
> Who else would soar above the view of men,
> And keep us all in servile fearfulness.

> (I.1.72–75)

Fearful is one of a cluster of key words that recur over and over again in I.2 and I.3. *Dangers/dangerous* appears in I.2.63, 78, 194, 195, 209; I.3.115 and I.3.124. The storm that terrifies Casca in Act I scene 3 is both a danger in itself and the pretext for a gathering of danger-bearing words. The night is *perilous* (I.3.47), *dreadful* (I.3.56, 73), *fearful* (I.3.126, 137), *terrible* (I.3.130). The stormy atmosphere reinforces the ambiguity of Cassius's reference to Caesar:

> A man no mightier than thyself or me,
> In personal action, yet prodigious grown,
> And fearful, as these strange eruptions are.
>
> (I.3.76–78)

Caesar is *fearful*, which is to say both 'frightening' and 'afraid'. The decisions he takes in the play reflect both the fearsomeness he possesses and the fear that possesses him.

Caesar has three main decisions to make during the course of the play:

1 to accept or reject the crown offered to him by Antony;
2 to go to the Senate House on the ides of March or to stay at home;
3 to pardon Publius Cimber or to uphold his sentence of exile.

Despite the importance of the considerations implicit in the first of these decisions, it is on the second that Shakespeare chooses to concentrate. In going to the meeting of the Senate, Caesar rejects the warnings and persuasions of the Soothsayer, Calphurnia, the augurers (II.2.38–40) and Artemidorus. He goes in fear, but he goes. Why? Apparently because Decius persuades him, as he had assured the conspirators he would:

> I can o'ersway him; for he loves to hear
> That unicorns may be betrayed with trees,
> And bears with glasses, elephants with holes,
> Lions with toils, and men with flatterers.
> But when I tell him he hates flatterers,
> He says he does, being then most flatterèd.
>
> (II.1.203–208)

In fact, Decius does no more than remind Caesar of his own priorities. Caesar is the master of the public gesture. He may, in the seclusion of his home, listen to Calphurnia's warnings, but he will forget them once he is reminded of his public status, and before the Senate itself, he will brush Artemidorus aside: 'What touches us ourself shall be last served' (III.1.7). The private Caesar does not exist in public, as Decius is shrewd enough to recognise. The soldier-statesman who was for so long the master of his public image has, at the moment of crucial decision, become its slave. In this sense, Caesar makes the clinching contribution to his own downfall. But there is, of course, an irony. It is the private Caesar that the conspirators succeed in killing: the public image, the spirit of Caesar, lives on and will eventually overwhelm Cassius and Brutus.

Caesar conducts his politics in public (and dies as a result). Brutus conducts his in private, too (and dies as a result). It is Brutus's greatness and also the source of his weakness that he can understand politics only by analogy with the conduct of his own life. His major decisions during the course of the play are:

1 to join in the assassination plot;
2 to spare Antony's life;
3 to allow Antony to speak at Caesar's funeral;
4 to rebuke Cassius for moral flexibility;
5 to march at once to Philippi;
6 to commit suicide.

Despite the widely differing nature of these decisions, they are all taken in similar terms. That is to say that they are all justified or explained by reference to an ideal *individual* code of morals. Where Caesar made his private decisions according to public criteria, Brutus makes his public decisions according to private criteria. Thus, even a decision so purely military as that affecting the timing of the march to Philippi is glossed (glossed *over*, Cassius might reasonably have claimed in retrospect) by a quasi-philosophical metaphor:

> There is a tide in the affairs of men,
> Which, taken at the flood, leads on to fortune;
> Omitted, all the voyage of their life
> Is bound in shallows and in miseries.

(IV.3.216–219)

It is the first of Brutus's decisions on which Shakespeare chooses to place the greatest emphasis. The man we first see is already 'Vexèd . . . with passions of some difference' (I.2.39–40) when Cassius begins to edge him towards the conspiracy. Cassius's initial approach, the attack on Caesar as an individual, is largely ineffective. Brutus is evidently too high-minded to succumb to jealousy. Cassius moves on to appeal to family pride:

> There was a Brutus once that would have brooked
> Th'eternal devil to keep his state in Rome
> As easily as a king.

(I.2.159–161)

Brutus shows clearer signs of interest now, but we cannot be sure that Cassius's blandishments are the cause of it. He is doing no more than reminding Brutus of thoughts that were already in his mind. It would seem, at this stage, that Brutus needs a political incentive as distinct from a personal one in order to convince himself of the rightness of conspiring against Caesar. His interrogation of Casca about the offering of the crown to Caesar is part of his pursuit for a self-persuading pretext for taking political action against tyranny. But Caesar has rejected the offer and Brutus remains pensively undecided. Cassius, however, is notably more confident, at the end of Act I scene 2, that Brutus can be won over to the conspiracy. The wording of his plan for the further persuading of his friend is intriguing. His closing soliloquy begins cynically:

> Well, Brutus, thou art noble; yet I see
> Thy honourable metal may be wrought
> From that it is disposed: therefore it is meet
> That noble minds keep ever with their likes;
> For who so firm that cannot be seduced?

(I.2.305–309)

But, despite his confidence, Cassius knows that there is still work to be done, and he knows very well the significance of Brutus's decision. Such is the authority of Brutus's name in Rome that he will virtually *create* the conspiracy by *joining* it. Cassius has only one significant advantage over Brutus, a down-to-earth belief that the end justifies the means. While Brutus ponders loftily, Cassius works on details:

> I will this night,
> In several hands, in at his windows throw,
> As if they came from several citizens,

Writings, all tending to the great opinion
That Rome holds of his name; wherein obscurely
Caesar's ambition shall be glancèd at.

(I.2.312–317)

We may wish to question the ultimate reliability of Cassius's opinion, but we cannot doubt his meaning. Whatever the eventual cause of Brutus's decision to join the conspiracy, Cassius places more reliance on an appeal to his pride than to his politics. The forged letters will refer only 'obscurely' to Caesar's ambition; their chief concern will be to flatter Brutus.

If Cassius is wrong about Brutus, the famous soliloquy at the opening of Act II scene 1 ought to prove it: but this soliloquy is one of the most confusing set pieces in the whole of Shakespeare's work. Brutus begins with a conclusion ('It must be by his death', II.1.10) and proceeds, rather hesitantly, to argue towards it. The argument is, in fact, notably unconvincing. Logic demands that Brutus should be saying: 'Caesar is already tyrannical. If he is crowned, and his tyranny thereby fully approved, it can only increase. Therefore, he must be killed.' The actual argument is quite different. To take just the concluding lines:

And, since the quarrel
Will bear no colour for the thing he is,
Fashion it thus: that what he is, augmented,
Would run to these and these extremities;
And therefore think him as a serpent's egg
Which, hatched, would, as his kind, grow mischievous,
And kill him in the shell.

(II.1.28–34)

What Brutus argues is this: 'Caesar is *not* at present tyrannical. Therefore, in order to reach the conclusion with which I started (i.e. 'It must be by his death'), I will take as a hypothesis that he would become tyrannical if he were crowned, and kill him for that reason.' Brutus's willingness to pronounce a virtual sentence of death on the grounds of a hypothesis that is absolutely incapable of proof is neither intellectually nor morally respectable. The kinder conclusion is that, despite the opening imperative, Brutus has not yet decided, that he is simply rehearsing the arguments that might lead to a decision. But, in that case, when is the decision made? There is nothing special about the letter Brutus opens at line 45:

> Such instigations have been often dropped
> Where I have took them up.

and the same evasion of the indicative mood that characterises the soliloquy is present in the conditional resolution that follows the reading of the letter:

> O Rome, I make thee promise,
> If the redress will follow, thou receivest
> Thy full petition at the hand of Brutus.

(II.1.56–58)

It seems to be on the strength of an 'if' that Brutus determines to kill Caesar. His actual joining of the conspiracy is not confirmed until after his conversation 'aside' with Cassius, which takes place during the ten lines (II.1.101–111) when Decius, Cinna and Casca are trying to work out where the sun rises. This is a quite extraordinary moment. The decision on which the whole play turns is being taken at the side or the back of the stage and *we cannot hear it*. Shakespeare has chosen to give us instead ten lines of inconsequential fractiousness. I am not suggesting that, during these ten lines, Cassius succeeds in persuading Brutus to kill Caesar, but rather that Shakespeare did not (could not? would not?) put into Brutus's part any convincing reason for his agreeing to become the murderer of his political leader and sometime friend. It is not impossible that he was unable to reconcile the character he had created with the actions of the historical Brutus. But there is another explanation. Act II scene 1 is a carefully constructed scene of moral choice, almost a play-within-a-play modelled on the ethical debates of the sixteenth-century Morality plays. Shakespeare, according to this explanation, intends to leave the audience in no doubt that Brutus's decision is falsely based.

It is not necessary that we should prefer any single interpretation of this complex scene to any other, although the actor of Brutus may find that his problems start there. The fact is that virtually every decision Brutus makes is a mistake. Even the decision to tax Cassius with moral flexibility is compromised if, as seems unavoidable, we recognise the flimsiness of Brutus's own moral stance. Shakespeare recognised, more fully even than Plutarch, the fascination of a political conflict between a good leader and a good man. The historical account of Caesar's death provided a choice example of this opposition. Shakespeare was excited by it, and *Julius Caesar* records that excitement. Caesar and Brutus share a prime concern for the fortunes of Rome. They also acknowledge, Brutus more painfully than Caesar, that, in the existing circumstances, all their own choices are choices made on behalf of Rome. The making of decisions in a context of extreme danger constitutes almost the whole of their activity in the play.

AFTERTHOUGHTS

1

Explain the importance to his argument of Thomson's initial focus on the word 'fearful' (pages 58–59).

2

Why do you think Shakespeare chose not to present directly Caesar's feelings about the offer of a crown (page 59)?

3

Do you agree with Thomson's contention that 'where Caesar made his private decisions according to public criteria, Brutus makes his public decisions according to private criteria' (page 60)?

4

Do you agree with Thomson's suggestion about why Brutus's final decision to join the conspiracy comes as an unheard conversational 'aside' (page 63)?

Michael Mangan
*Michael Mangan lectures in English at
Sheffield University, and is the author of
numerous critical studies.*

ESSAY

'I am no orator': the language of public spaces

In *Julius Caesar* two kinds of space are set in opposition to each other. There are the private spaces, like Brutus's orchard or Caesar's house, where a man may be alone with his musings or his fears, where he may speak his most unacceptable thoughts, and even his treasonable ones. And yet these private spaces are comparatively few. Even those that do exist frequently become public — as Caesar's house does as it fills with his friends, advisers, ministers and counsellors. In modern productions of the play, set designers offer audiences architecture and vistas which announce the public face of the city of Rome — so much so that the critical cliché that Rome itself is a major character in the play seems well-founded. Thus *Julius Caesar* presents itself as a very public play; the spaces in which significant events occur are public ones: streets, squares and, later, battlefields. Occasionally people will gather in the corner of such places and whisper to each other secret and dangerous things, but more often characters bow to the nature of the places they inhabit, and speak in the public languages demanded by their environment.

Of these spaces, the most public is the market-place: of the speeches in the play the most public are those spoken in the market-place by Brutus and Antony, as they address the crowd, the Plebeians of Rome after Caesar's death. Act III scene 2 is a long and apparently static scene: it contains one crowd and two lectures: Brutus and Antony get up into a 'pulpit', they talk to a crowd, and then they come down again. Yet this apparent stasis is deceptive; in many ways III.2 is the most dynamic scene in the play, the one containing the greatest amount of movement. It is, however, a movement which takes place not in physical terms, but in the hearts and minds of the listeners, the people of Rome.

Language spoken with the express aim of moving or persuading is called rhetoric, and we know that rhetoric was one of the core subjects of the Elizabethan schoolchild's national curriculum. The debate between Brutus and Mark Antony is a self-consciously rhetorical exercise, which Brutus sets up a couple of scenes earlier when, against the advice of his co-conspirators, he allows Mark Antony to speak at Caesar's funeral:

> You shall not in your funeral speech blame us,
> But speak all good you can devise of Caesar,
> And say you do't by our permission;
> Else you shall not have any hand at all
> About his funeral. And you shall speak
> In the same pulpit whereto I am going,
> After my speech is ended.

(III.1.245–251)

That, then, is the task: to say nothing against the conspirators, and to speak to a crowd already primed by Brutus. Shakespeare seems to be setting himself a challenge: with those constraints, can Mark Antony plausibly sway the Roman people? Of course he can — and we watch and applaud the skill with which he does it.

The two big speeches in III.2 constitute a rhetorical set-piece, as formal in its way as the speeches in a courtroom drama. It is Brutus who speaks first — to a crowd who are puzzled, confused and rather hostile: 'We will be satisfied: let us be satisfied', they are shouting as the scene opens. They are also, however, eager to listen to Brutus. He has no trouble getting them to hear him. We remember the conspirators' initial reasons

for wanting Brutus on their side, because of the 'opinion . . .
which every noble Roman bears of [him]' (II.1.92–93). Brutus's
reputation as a man of honour ensures him a hearing even from
this crowd, who only recently had been acclaiming the man
whom Brutus has just killed. This last detail should not be
forgotten: when Brutus addresses the crowd, he is potentially in
danger. It is vital that his rhetoric should be effective: the crowd
otherwise may tear him apart.

> Romans, countrymen, and lovers, hear me for my cause, and be
> silent, that you may hear. Believe me for mine honour, and have
> respect to mine honour, that you may believe. Censure me in
> your wisdom, and awake your senses, that you may the better
> judge.
>
> (lines 13–17)

If one meaning of the word 'rhetoric' is 'language whose design
is to persuade', another connected meaning is 'the use or study of
the ornaments of speech of eloquence'. In this sense, too, Brutus's
speech is a highly rhetorical one. And while it would be deeply
tedious to go through Brutus's speeches like some kind of literary
train-spotter, noting down examples of *commoratio, auxesis* or
anacoenosis, it is, nonetheless worth looking at the way that
Brutus patterns his language in order to suggest, both consciously and subliminally, certain attitudes and conclusions.
For, like any good politician, Brutus knows that fine-sounding,
well-balanced sentences are an invaluable tool in the gentle art
of persuading people to accept your point of view:

hear . . .   my cause . . .   AND *. . . be silent*
believe . . . mine honour . . . AND *. . . mine honour*
censure . . . wisdom . . .   AND *. . . senses*

that you may ... *hear*
that you may ... *believe*
that you may ... *judge*

That pivotal 'AND' allows for a progression of rhetorical subtlety.
These three sentences are linked together by virtue of their similarity of structure. When sentences are linked in such a way
there is a kind of transference of plausibility: if the first sentence makes sense, the listener is that much more inclined to

assume that the second and the third will too. And Brutus's first sentence does indeed make sense, since it is a plea for some quiet so that he can speak. It is fairly straightforward, but it also begins a sequence in which meaning is created by repetition of key words and phrases. The first sentence merely has clauses which balance by virtue of beginning and ending with the same word. The second sentence makes rather less sense than the first. It seems to offer a progression but in fact it is quite circular: it actually means nothing more than 'believe me because you know you can believe me'. The third sentence makes the repetitions within it work even harder. It starts and ends with the idea of judging (or censuring), but through an assonance between the words 'censure' and 'senses' links this with an appeal to the Romans' 'senses' (including presumably their common sense) which is in turn linked with 'wisdom' — the word which stands in a corresponding position in what is by now a familiar verbal pattern. This sentence, far from being circular, is one which moves the listener from one implied position to another, from the negative connotations of 'censure' to the more positive ones of 'better judge'.

> If there be any in this assembly, any dear friend of Caesar's, to
> him I say that Brutus' love to Caesar was no less than his. If
> then that friend demand why Brutus rose against Caesar, this is
> my answer: not that I loved Caesar less, but that I loved Rome
> more.

> (lines 19–22)

This next movement of Brutus's speech perhaps *would* benefit from being described by its classical rhetorical name. *Procatalepsis* means the anticipating of an objection. These two sentences each anticipate the potential objections of a fictional 'dear friend of Caesar's'. '*If*' that friend question Brutus's love for Caesar, Brutus can affirm it. '*If*' that friend question Brutus's actions, Brutus has an answer. This answer is a crucial one, for it introduces the essential equation of Brutus's speech:

NOT
loved   Caesar   less
BUT
loved   Rome   more

Brutus's central task in this speech is to separate out Rome from Caesar, to portray the interests of Rome (and thus, by implication, the interests of his listeners) as being in opposition to the interests of Caesar. He needs to make his listeners believe, as he does, that Caesar and Rome were inherently inimical to each other. Much of the rhetoric of the rest of this speech is aimed at performing this task:

> Had you rather Caesar were living, and die all slaves, than that Caesar were dead, to live all free men?
>
> (lines 22–24)

Once more the sense of an implied logical equation is inescapable. In fact, there are two equations implied in this sentence:

1 Caesar living = [Romans, listeners] die
  Caesar dead = [Romans, listeners] live

2 Caesar living = [Romans, listeners] all slaves
  Caesar dead = [Romans, listeners] all free men.

If he can once convince the Roman people that this equation is true, he will have succeeded in his task. This is the rhetorical centre of his address.

Like a canny hunter, having sighted his prey Brutus does not immediately rush after it. He seems, momentarily, to digress:

> As Caesar loved me, I weep for him; as he was fortunate, I rejoice at it; as he was valiant, I honour him; but, as he was ambitious, I slew him. There is tears for his love; joy for his fortune; honour for his valour; and death for his ambition.
>
> (lines 24–28)

The repeated sequence proclaims its own logic. Love leads to tears, fortune leads to joy, valour leads to honour and ambition leads to death. Brutus here is talking about his own personal response, but is couching that response in terms of a seemingly unquestionable sequence of causes and effects. This transmutation of the personal into the inexorable leads him to challenge his audience:

> Who is here so base that would be a bondman? If any, speak; for him have I offended. Who is here so rude that would not be a Roman? If any, speak; for him have I offended. Who is here so

vile that will not love his country? If any, speak; for him have I
offended. I pause for a reply.

(lines 28–34)

Small wonder that nobody does reply to his challenge, for
Brutus's questions are rhetorical in a further sense of that word:
they do not expect an answer. And since nobody in the crowd is
likely to claim to be base, rude or vile, it follows from Brutus's
own logic that he has offended nobody. Brutus's rhetoric has
proved, elegantly and persuasively, that the murder of Caesar
was not only justifiable but necessary; the crowd is his entirely.

Critics often characterise the crowds in Shakespeare's
Roman plays as fickle and easily swayed, and sometimes they
are. But the point should be made that this crowd has at least
been swayed by a brilliant orator: if they are persuaded, it is by
a master of persuasion. The reputation which Brutus has in
Rome as a genius of rhetoric is certainly substantiated within
the action of this scene. At the end of his speech, however,
Brutus makes an uncharacteristic tactical error. One of the most
basic rules of rhetoric is to make sure that you get in with the
last word. Yet Brutus — perhaps because he is an honourable
man, or perhaps because he is over-confident — says his piece
and then walks away, leaving the stage and the crowd to Mark
Antony. Not only that, he even allows Mark Antony to claim for
his own use a very important prop — the coffin which contains
Caesar's body.

Antony, it is true, needs all the help he can get, since the
success of Brutus's speech has left both him and Shakespeare
with an initial problem. Mark Antony's problem is that the
crowd are now very firmly persuaded to Brutus's point of view.
Shakespeare's problem is that he is writing a single scene which
demands two brilliant rhetorical performances in it. There is a
danger that it will simply appear that he's doing the same thing
twice over. Brutus's dense and intricate rhetoric cannot be
repeated; for Mark Antony's speech a different kind of technique
is required.

Although Mark Antony has his audience handed to him, as
it were, on a plate, he has difficulty getting started. The crowd
which he inherits are initially even more hostile towards him
than they had earlier been towards Brutus: we hear one of them

say, "'Twere best he speak no harm of Brutus here!' His first words are drowned in a babble of noise from the crowd, his address seems as if it will go unheard. It seems as if he has an impossible task. And yet, starting slowly, he begins to take apart Brutus's speech.

> The noble Brutus
> Hath told you Caesar was ambitious.
> If it were so, it was a grievous fault,
> And grievously hath Caesar answered it.
> Here, under leave of Brutus and the rest —
> For Brutus is an honourable man;
> So are they all, all honourable men —
> Come I to speak in Caesar's funeral.

(lines 78–85)

Brutus's rhetoric was calculated to build up a picture in which Caesar was equated with ambition, and opposed to the general good of Rome, whereas Brutus and his friends were to be seen as acting from honourable motives on behalf of the general good of Rome. By picking up on two words, 'honourable' and 'ambitious', Mark Antony's language works to undercut this picture.

> He was my friend, faithful and just to me;
> But Brutus says he was ambitious,
> And Brutus is an honourable man.
> He hath brought many captives home to Rome,
> Whose ransoms did the general coffers fill:
> Did this in Caesar seem ambitious?

(lines 86–91)

Mark Antony, already, is beginning to knit back together Caesar's aims and the general good of Rome: the captives' ransoms, he reminds his audience, went to fill up the general coffers — not Caesar's own private purse. The whole of this first part of his speech is aimed at providing a series of apparent 'proofs' that Caesar was not in fact ambitious at all.

In fact the evidence Mark Antony puts forward in order to disprove Caesar's ambition is not particularly strong. He argues, first that Caesar was a good friend to him, Mark Antony: however true this may be, it has little bearing on Caesar's ambition. Secondly, he makes his point about the captives' ransoms: proof, perhaps that Caesar was not personally avaricious, but not that he was not ambitious: ambition might well be served by such a gesture. Thirdly, Mark Antony argues that Caesar was moved to tears by the sight of poor people starving: again, it might say much about his compassion, but it says little about his ambition. Antony's strongest argument concerns the fact that Caesar was offered and refused the crown on the Lupercal. This does indeed seem to clinch Mark Antony's case — yet even this is not unambiguous. We remember Casca's account of the refusal: 'he put it by once; but for all that, to my thinking, he would fain have had it' (I.2.236–237).

But what is central to Mark Antony's speech is not the plausibility or otherwise of his proofs. It is the way he presents his case — once more, it is rhetoric which is the issue. Mark Antony is using language not to prove but to suggest. Moreover he is slowly dismantling Brutus's notion of Caesar's 'ambition'. Since he is giving specific examples of Caesar's behaviour, he can then question whether these actions are adequately accounted for by being labelled 'ambitious'. A word repeated over and over again begins to lose its meaning. As with 'ambitious', so with 'honourable': the more Mark Antony repeats that 'Brutus is an honourable man', the more he invites the crowd to repudiate him.

Antony's speech does not have the detailed craftsmanship of Brutus's, the alliterations and the balanced clauses. Mark Antony's is a rhetoric that appears to hide rhetoric; while being every bit as artful in construction as Brutus's speech, its task is to appear 'natural'. A central element in Mark Antony's strategy, in fact, is to set against Brutus's elegant rationalisations a personal, heartfelt, and apparently artless response to the death of Caesar. So, just as he had opened his speech with the simple fact of his own personal knowledge of Caesar, Mark Antony closes the first phase of his argument by returning to that fact:

> I speak not to disprove what Brutus spoke
> But here I am to speak what I do know.
> You all did love him once, not without cause;
> What cause withholds you then to mourn for him?
> O judgement! thou art fled to brutish beasts,
> And men have lost their reason. Bear with me;

My heart is in the coffin there with Caesar,
And I must pause till it come back to me.

(lines 101–108)

Caesar's body — the physical object there on the stage — will be used as a key reference point throughout Mark Antony's speech, one to which he will return with increasing force. At present he contents himself with drawing attention mainly to the coffin which contains it, but even so he is making a point: that for all Brutus's rhetoric, the reality of the deed involved the taking of another human being's life. Mark Antony does not attempt to disprove Brutus's words; he merely sets them in the context of other realities: the dead body of Caesar, and his, Antony's, knowledge of him when he was alive. He speaks to the emotions, while simultaneously invoking his listeners' judgement and their reason. He exhorts the crowd to feel their own grief at Caesar's death, he loses his temper with them, and is himself so overcome with emotion that he has to break off his speech. We remember, by contrast, how *un*emotional Brutus's oration had been: its appeal was entirely to the intellect. If Brutus's speech made explicit a series of logical corollaries concerning Caesar and Rome, Mark Antony, much more subtly, is implicitly suggesting another corollary: that Brutus spoke merely words whereas he, Antony, speaks with the voice of truth and of feeling — which, he implies, leaves him so moved that he cannot continue with his speech.

When he does continue, it is to a crowd who are now beginning to warm to him. Still harping on the word 'honourable', he begins to play his trump card — the slow and tantalising uncovering of a key piece of information. Like a fictional detective he teases his audience with the vital piece of evidence which he knows and they do not — the contents of Caesar's will:

Let but the commons hear this testament,
Which, pardon me, I do not mean to read,
And they would go and kiss dead Caesar's wounds,
And dip their napkins in his sacred blood,
Yea, beg a hair of him for memory,
And, dying, mention it within their wills,
Bequeathing it as a rich legacy
Unto their issue.

(lines 131–138)

The speech unrolls like a fugue: a new theme is stated, that of the will, but old themes are kept alive and developed at the same time. The material presence of Caesar's body is referred to again, as Mark Antony directs his hearers' thoughts once more towards the reality of the dead man who lies in the coffin before them. It is as if he is cutting away the covering of justifications which Brutus had offered, and is allowing them to see afresh the awfulness of the murder. But by now Caesar's body is referred to as more than just a mortal corpse: it is spoken of as if it were the body of a martyred saint, with its 'sacred blood' and its relics of hair. And then, in a final elegant movement, Antony brings the images full circle, re-introducing wills and legacies. The crowd react predictably, demanding to see Caesar's will, but still Antony delays. Typically, in his response he simultaneously reveals and conceals:

> It is not meet you know how Caesar loved you.
> You are not wood, you are not stones, but men;
> And being men, hearing the will of Caesar,
> It will inflame you, it will make you mad.
> 'Tis good you know not that you are his heirs;
> For if you should, O, what would come of it?
>
> (lines 142–147)

Even as he pretends to keep it from them, he tells them what he wants them to know: that Caesar loved them and that they are his heirs. By now the crowd are almost at fever pitch: one more mention of the word 'honourable' has them snarling, 'They were villains, murderers!' The demand to see the will is Antony's cue to descend from the pulpit, to make the significant movement down to join with the crowd and thereby announce his unity with them. It is a move for which his rhetoric has prepared him throughout. Brutus's language was always that of the orator, standing above the throng and speaking down to it. Antony's is that most insidious of rhetoric — the rhetoric which masquerades as plain speech. And so this master of manipulation takes his place in among the crowd and continues his consummate playing upon their emotions. Dropping for a while the theme of the will, he concentrates once more upon the physical details of the murder. He recreates it all, and at first he does so at one remove, using Caesar's mantle as a visual aid in his roll-call of the chief conspirators:

> Look, in this place ran Cassius' dagger through;
> See what a rent the envious Casca made;
> Through this, the well-belovèd Brutus stabbed
>
> . . .
>
> O, now you weep, and I perceive you feel
> The dint of pity. These are gracious drops.
> Kind souls, what weep you when you but behold
> Our Caesar's vesture wounded? Look you here,
> Here is himself, marred, as you see, with traitors.
>
> (lines 175–177, 194–198)

By the time he finally directs their attention to the body itself, he does not need to hide behind equivocation, but calls them traitors outright. The crowd by now are all set to riot, with cries of 'Revenge! About! Seek! Burn! Fire! Kill! Slay!' But Antony is taking no chances. Having brought off a *tour de force* of persuasive speaking, he then shamelessly disavows any rhetorical skill, conjuring up instead the gruesome image of the mutilated body which becomes a mouth:

> I am no orator, as Brutus is,
> But, as you know me all, a plain blunt man,
> That love my friend; and that they know full well
> That gave me public leave to speak of him.
> For I have neither wit, nor words, nor worth,
> Action, nor utterance, nor the power of speech
> To stir men's blood; I only speak right on.
> I tell you that which you yourselves do know,
> Show you sweet Caesar's wounds, poor poor dumb mouths,
> And bid them speak for me.
>
> (lines 218–227)

There is, of course, a mixture of truth and falsity in what Antony says here. It is true that Antony's central strategy has been to bid Caesar's wounds to speak for him, to awaken the crowd's awareness of the reality of Caesar's death. It is equally true that this task is one which requires the height of oratorical powers to accomplish. This moment is typical not only of Antony but of Shakespeare: in calling attention to a supposed lack of art, he makes an audience momentarily aware of his own artistry. Nor has Antony finished. The crowd have been kept at boiling point for several minutes, but now, finally, Antony reads them the will — the will which they had almost forgotten in their anger!

> To every Roman citizen he gives,
> To every several man, seventy-five drachmas.
> . . .
> Moreover he hath left you all his walks,
> His private arbours, and new-planted orchards,
> On this side Tiber; he hath left them you,
> And to your heirs for ever
>
> (lines 242–243, 248–251)

The argument comes full circle and the point is finally, undisputably, made: each member of the crowd is now totally convinced that Caesar was not personally ambitious, but had at heart the general good of 'every Roman citizen'. Not a shred remains of Brutus's carefully constructed argument. And of course it is quite fitting that the final proof which Antony offers of Caesar's integrity should be this bequest of his arbours and orchards — the transmutation of private land into public spaces.

AFTERTHOUGHTS

1

Explain the significance of the title of this essay.

2

Consider Mangan's analysis of Brutus's speech in the market-place (pages 67–71) in the light of Campbell's view that 'his haughty address to the Roman mob shows him neglecting his powers of oratory when they are most needed' (page 85). What is *your* assessment of Brutus's performance?

3

What differences does Mangan highlight between Brutus's and Antony's approaches (pages 72–74)?

4

Explain the 'mixture of truth and falsity' Mangan identifies in Antony's words to the crowd (page 76). Would it be fair to say that this same mixture has characterised his speech throughout the play?

Patrick Campbell

Patrick Campbell is Principal Lecturer in English at Middlesex Polytechnic. He is the author of a number of studies and articles, and edits a journal (MDT) of the Performance Arts.

ESSAY

Brutus: 'Noblest Roman of them all'?

Analysing characters in a play is less straightforward than you might imagine. Though the leading players must attract our attention if we are to continue to watch or read, these representations will inevitably be partial ones. Odd then that dramatic convention actually allows *more* exposure of particular facets of character — certainly in relation to the central figures — than is often the case with real people. We cannot, for example, read the minds of our friends, still less get inside the heads of strangers, in the way Shakespeare can those of his 'dramatis personae'. For while the dramatist explores personality in straightforward ways — through the opinions of others, or by the public statements and everyday social behaviour of his creations, he is able to concentrate on the significant moments in both their outer and inner lives. In so doing, Shakespeare follows two important principles — first, that our essential nature is most glaringly exposed in moments of crisis, in what may even be life-or-death situations; second, that we rarely reveal our most private thoughts to anyone but ourselves. Thus, by placing his protagonists in testing circumstances, Shakespeare reveals the well-springs of character through action. And by making them shun company and talk to themselves, he allows us privileged access to their most intimate feelings, to appreciate the great divide that frequently separates what people think and what they say.

We will consider how Shakespeare uses these 'tricks of the trade' in relation to Brutus. But first we must clarify his status in the play. If we accept the 'evidence' of the title, for example, Brutus is not the central figure, the protagonist of the play. Nonetheless, Shakespeare does his utmost to ensure that it is Brutus who captures our attention from first to last Act, to convince us that he is the hub around which the action revolves, and that his complex personality is the most fascinating aspect of *Julius Caesar*. Caesar himself, a political and military genius on the evidence both of history and Mark Antony, is allotted a mere 140 lines — and pretty drab ones at that — in a play which eliminates him from the action before Act III scene 2. Brutus, on the other hand, Antony's oratory apart, dominates almost from beginning to end. From Caesar's early judgement that 'he sits high in all the people's hearts' (I.3.157) to Antony's closing epitaph, we are constantly made aware of his magnetic presence. The play is a 'tragedy' (Shakespeare's own word) because it involves the overthrow of the established political order. But it is also a tragedy in *human* terms because it charts the sudden rise and equally abrupt decline and fall of 'the noblest Roman', a man whose obsession with principle is at once his noblest attribute and greatest source of frailty.

To paint as complete a picture of Brutus as possible in the space of at most three hours, Shakespeare employs a range of dramatic procedures. Initially, for example, Brutus is seen largely through the eyes of observers and especially the scheming Cassius. He believes that Brutus's envy of Caesar and his distaste for tyranny can be so exploited that even his 'honourable mettle may be wrought/ From that it is disposed' (I.2.306–307). Indeed Cassius, aware of Brutus's tight-lipped reactions to his initial overtures, promises to be a mirror for his thoughts:

> ·   I, your glass,
> Will modestly discover to yourself
> That of yourself which you yet know not of.

(I.2.68–70)

Events render his promise superfluous, for Brutus, after a period of inner debate, takes decisive action and quickly moves centre stage. But our interest in him is whetted as we seek to find out the truth of Cassius's character assessment. The clues arrive in various forms. From the onset Brutus has been brooding and introspective. When he admits to Cassius that he is 'not game-some' (I.2.28), it is not only an insight into his innately serious nature but an admission that he is presently a worried and tormented man. As he himself admits, he is 'with himself at war' and consequently 'Forgets the shows/ of love to other men' (I.2.46–47).

The early scenes continue to highlight this inner tension, hint at its source and show its resolution. If the external catalyst in this process is Cassius, the ultimate decision to go ahead must be taken by Brutus and him alone. But at first his response is too guarded to be true. Flattered by the suggestion that '"Brutus" will start a spirit as soon as "Caesar"' (I.2.146), the self-conscious rhetoric of his overt reaction is an indication — and one that Shakespeare's audience would undoubtedly have spotted — that Brutus is deliberately hiding his real feelings and buying time before committing himself to 'such high things'. All he *will* admit is 'What you would work me to, I have some aim' (I.2.162). It is only at the end of this speech, as Cassius recognises, that a 'show/ Of fire' hints at his growing emotional involvement (I.2.175–176).

But when Brutus is alone his most intimate thoughts are allowed expression. Here the aside, and more particularly its extended form the soliloquy, are employed as sophisticated dramatic devices — not only to articulate secret ambitions and fears but to reveal the very processes whereby tensions are explored, examined and perhaps resolved. For Brutus, as for Macbeth, these conflicts are so intensely experienced that they threaten to tear him apart, a fact which Portia is not slow to recognise. It is a potent source of dramatic irony that we, as readers or audience, know more about the nature of this inner debate than a devoted wife — who can recognise the symptoms without knowing the causes of his 'sick offence within' (II.1.268).

In Brutus's first soliloquy, fittingly in the sanctuary of his orchard, he muses on one of Shakespeare's perennial preoccupations — the theme of ambition and the effect of power on personality ('It is the bright day that brings forth the adder', II.1.14). What this reveals about Brutus is not just a capacity for pronouncing on human nature in general, but a dawning realisation that the embryo snake (Caesar) must be killed 'in the shell' before it can 'grow mischievous' (II.1.33). But the next soliloquy shows he is still appalled by the prospect of murder and fearful of its possible consequences, still balancing the competing claims of loyalty to his leader against his sense of honour and justice, perhaps conscious too of a lurking personal ambition. His words, like those of Macbeth before the killing of Duncan, stress this divided 'state of man'. The image, a familiar one in Shakespeare, is that of the 'microcosm' or little world of a mind at odds with itself. Like a 'kingdom' lacking clear direction, it 'suffers then/ The nature of an insurrection' (II.1.68–69).

The final reflection reveals that the irrevocable decision has been taken. Henceforth Brutus must conceal his true feelings, 'Hide . . . in smiles and affability' the 'monstrous visage' of assassination (II.1.82, 81). Under the spotlight, he must seek the shadows. When the conspirators arrive at his house, appropriately in darkness, Brutus takes the initiative. A natural leader, he warms to the collective endeavour. He needs no more convincing; he is an idealist pursuing a just cause:

> What need we any spur but our own cause
> To prick us to redress?

> (II.1.123–124)

A Roman for whom honour is all, his anticipatory vision is one of purgation, not murder; the act of assassination will be a ritual blood-letting that will heal the body politic of Rome.

The bloody deed is speedily accomplished, its most poignant moment Caesar's dying '*Et tu, Brute?*', testimony to his surprise that Brutus, of *all* people, should be implicated. Even Caesar has the highest regard for him. But he is steeped in blood now, and soul-searching soliloquies will be things of the past. Now Shakespeare will let us judge his single-minded protagonist by his public bearing in crisis situations.

To his credit Brutus remains, as he did in the Senate scene, calm and dignified. But Fortune's wheel is already turning against him. Unable or unwilling to gauge the feelings of the mob, he delivers a stiff and abstract speech (Shakespeare deliberately puts it in *prose*) and is rapidly upstaged by Mark Antony's impassioned oratory and deft manipulation of the mob's hunger for melodrama (the bloody corpse) and money (Caesar's will). Forced to flee the city, Brutus nonetheless shows in adversity the same unyielding concern for principle. His courage never deserts him, his belief in his own incorruptibility never flags. Before the decisive action at Philippi he seems almost to welcome death, confiding to Cassius:

> ... think not, thou noble Roman,
> That ever Brutus will go bound to Rome;
> He bears too great a mind.
>
> (V.1.110–112)

This self-styled 'noble Roman' is determined to die like a hero. Defeated by Octavius, his only course of action is to impale himself on his sword, thereby achieving 'honour by his death' (V.5.57) and deserving of Antony's tribute.

Brutus then *is* the play's protagonist, not only the axis around which the public events of conspiracy, assassination and civil war revolve, but also, it is safe to assume, the personality that most exercised Shakespeare's imagination. He is, psychologically and morally, as well as dramatically and politically, at the centre of *Julius Caesar*. But is he, as most critics have argued, a hero?

In seeking the answer, a useful starting point is North's translation of Plutarch's *Life of Brutus*. It was, after all the source which Shakespeare himself used and adapted. From Plutarch we learn that Brutus was 'framed unto virtue' and 'gentle and constant'. His arch-enemy in former times, Caesar now 'kept him always about him' and did 'as much honour and esteem him as any man in his company'. Plutarch goes on to enthuse over his special qualities — his immunity to flattery ('an upright mind') and a commitment to justice and truth that sometimes issued in 'a kind of forcible and vehement persuasion that calmed not till he has obtained his desire'. So 'well-beloved' a man killed Caesar, Plutarch concludes, not out of 'private malice or envy' but 'as thinking the act commendable of itself'[1].

If Plutarch believed the historical figure of Brutus to be the

---

[1] *Shakespeare's Plutarch*, ed. W Skeat, London, 1875, pp. 105–130.

stuff of story-book heroes, almost all these positive aspects were also fascinating enough for Shakespeare to incorporate in his own dramatic portrait. Indeed, critics have usually found in Shakespeare's Brutus a total endorsement of Antony's 'the noblest Roman of them all'. Dover Wilson in the introduction to the New Cambridge edition (1949) offers a strongly pro-Brutus assessment, Peter Alexander talks of a play 'startlingly calculated to favour Brutus' at Caesar's expense[2], and Mark Van Doren of 'an exemplary gentleman[3]'. But this authorial favouritism — if it exists — does not blind Shakespeare to his faults. In the context of a *tragedy* it must be thus. For Brutus, like Macbeth or Othello, represents *flawed* greatness; he is a man whose apparent virtues actually make him vulnerable and contribute to his downfall. If he has the capacity for heroism, he also has the capacity for self-destruction. Antony, we must not forget, can *afford* to be generous in victory (he described Brutus earlier as one of 'these butchers', III.1.255). But Shakespeare wants to probe more deeply than any adversary into the enigma that is Brutus.

Not that we should underestimate his nobility. That Brutus achieves tragic status — or comes close to it — is a direct consequence of the respect he commands, from friend, foe and audience alike. Right from the start he impresses as a man of honour, inwardly wrestling with his conscience, outwardly inspiring loyalty in his friends. To use a fashionable word he has 'charisma'. As proof of her undying devotion, his wife wounds herself in the thigh; Caius Ligarius hero-worships at his feet:

> I am not sick if Brutus have in hand
> Any exploit worthy the name of honour

(II.1.316–317)

Brutus then is clearly a born leader of men. While it is Cassius who moots the idea of conspiracy, it is Brutus that everyone wants to mastermind the operation. Once won over, he assumes a commanding posture — as to the manner born. Admittedly he is conveniently close to Caesar, a fact not lost on Cassius as he

---

[2] *A Shakespeare Primer*, London, 1951, p. 93.
[3] *Shakespeare*, New York, 1955, p. 152.

privately reflects that 'Caesar doth bear me hard; but he loves Brutus' (I.2.310). But he is singled out for a more compelling all-round reason — his celebrated integrity, his absolute commitment to what he believes in. Using a metaphor from alchemy, Casca argues that Brutus's presence will transmute what people will regard as base motives for murder 'to virtue and to worthiness' (I.3.160). Cassius also knows that once he is convinced of the justice of the conspiracy, there will be no back-sliding. In the clandestine and murky meeting with the other conspirators, Brutus is assured that:

> . . . no man here
> But honours you; and every one doth wish
> You had but that opinion of yourself
> Which every noble Roman bears of you.

(II.1.90–93)

That word 'honour' follows him like a spoor through the events of the play. In Mark Antony's rabble-rousing speech there are nine ringing and increasingly sardonic reiterations of 'honourable'. Four are arrows aimed directly at the heart of Brutus. Though *we* retain our conviction that he is a man of his word, the fickle mob are remorselessly persuaded of his *dishonourable* motives. It is a rich and dramatically effective irony that the integrity of *Brutus* — of all things — should be an object of general suspicion.

Cassius's just-quoted judgement of Brutus, as *apparently* direct and positive as Antony's is sarcastic and negative, is also a piece of calculated flattery. It is true that everyone respects him, but Brutus does possess, as Cassius secretly suspects, a self-righteous belief in his own imperishable sense of honour. Indeed one could argue that it already threatens to become an obsession that will increasingly blind him to banal but needful practicalities and eventually lead him into a 'cul-de-sac' and defeat.

That Brutus is a poet with an ear for the resounding phrase and an eye for the vivid image certainly helps to persuade the conspirators of his unsullied motives. But even this gift does not always work to his advantage. Sadly for Brutus his haughty address to the Roman mob shows him neglecting his powers of oratory when they are most needed. Moreover, his fine phrases frequently conceal a refusal to face the facts. 'Let us be sacrificers, but not butchers', he reminds his fellow-plotters:

> Let's carve him as a dish fit for the gods,
> Not hew him as a carcass fit for hounds.

(II.1.173–174)

What Brutus forgets in his idealistic outburst is that murder in any shape or form is a cruel and messy business, not a religious rite. In any case, people who commit assassinations in public are unlikely to have time to stand back and admire their handiwork. Before Philippi, the second major *political* event of the play, Brutus utters a call to arms that would inspire the faintest of hearts:

> There is a tide in the affairs of men,
> Which, taken at the flood, leads on to fortune

(IV.3.216–217)

But what we need to remember is that this speech follows hard on his rejection of Cassius's sensible strategy. It is stirring poetry but in the context of an imminent battle it is bad advice. No one understands this capacity in Brutus for self-delusion, for verbal rationalising, better than Antony. His angry rejoinder in his final confrontation with Brutus may be a point-scoring one, but it nonetheless rings true:

> In your bad strokes, Brutus, you give good words;
> Witness the hole you made in Caesar's heart,
> Crying, 'Long live! Hail, Caesar!'

(V.1.30–32)

This conviction of his own rightness (a point we recall made by Plutarch) also renders Brutus unwilling or unable to embrace the opinions of friends whose motives he believes to be less valid or worthy than his own. While we may sometimes anticipate such inflexibility in great leaders, we lose all sympathy with the petulant Brutus when he quarrels with Cassius in his private tent. His high-handed denunciation of his friend for having an 'itchy palm' is made all the most unpalatable by his smug and priggish reference to his own purity of motive:

There is no terror, Cassius, in your threats;
For I am armed so strong in honesty
That they pass by me as the idle wind,
Which I respect not.

(IV.3.66–69)

It is a clear if not an appealing demonstration of how Stoic gentlemen should conduct themselves, but it does not win our hearts, still less battles. A least three times in the play, Brutus rejects sound advice — twice with disastrous consequences. The first occasion — when he spurns the conspirators' suggestion to involve Cicero the famous orator — is only *potentially* hazardous. Not so the twin decisions to dismiss thoughts of eliminating Antony ('so well beloved of Caesar', II.1.156), and to overrule the sensible delaying tactics proposed by Cassius and thereby lose field advantage at Philippi. Antony, one of whose roles in the play is to act as a commentator on Brutus, is not slow to recognise in this 'bull-at-a gate' strategy the courageous but tactically inept hand of Brutus, an adversary determined to:

. . . come down
With fearful bravery, thinking by this face
To fasten in our thoughts that they have courage

(V.1.9–11)

Antony's observation embraces a typically Shakespearean view — that in the world if *realpolitik* it is the hard-headed and adaptable leader, the 'street-wise guy', who usually outwits the idealist. Brutus not only omits to murder Antony when he has the chance, he compounds the error by granting his request to 'speak in the order of his funeral', (III.1.230), and then high-handedly neglects to stay and censor Antony's inflammatory speech to the mob. Such oversights cost him dear. They may be more admirable actions than the Machiavellian execution of a hundred Senators whom Octavius and Antony can only suspect of plot involvement, but the choices Brutus makes are, in practical terms, totally misguided. Antony, we recall, saves his skin by claiming he *will* be pals if the conspirators justify their deed. Such duplicity is not only alien to an honourable and absolute Brutus, it puts him at a disadvantage when dealing with the likes of Antony.

Brutus then is short-sighted and inflexible — increasingly so. As he arrogantly confides to Cassius, he 'bears too great a mind' to ever 'go bound to Rome' (V.1.112, 111). But his faults stop a long way short of the villainy of a Macbeth. So why, one wonders, does Brutus ever consent to join a bunch of assassins? Even Plutarch is evasive here. The only explicit reason offered by Shakespeare is Brutus's conviction that Caesar's rule is a 'high-sighted tyranny' (II.1.118). But we are given no specific examples of misrule to justify this judgement. What we *can* reasonably assume is that deep down Brutus harbours more personal motives, a profound dislike of Caesar, a wish to live up to the highest traditions of his own ancestors, perhaps an ambition to rule the greatest empire on earth. To be bracketed by Cassius with 'petty men' and 'underlings' (I.2.135, 140) clearly touches a raw nerve. All Brutus's talk of sacrifice and 'honesty to honesty engaged' (I.1.127) cannot blind us to the fact — one particularly distasteful to an Elizabethan audience — that he initiates an act of 'bloody treason' (III.2.193) and by murdering its acclaimed head threatens the very security of the state and its citizens.

I am conscious that I have stressed the shortcomings of Brutus. But this approach is, I believe, justified both to reveal those aspects of character which contribute to his undoing and to offer an antidote to critical assessments which, following Plutarch's portrayal and Antony's epitaph, have discovered in him unstained purity of motive and behaviour. Nonetheless, in the final analysis, we do remember and respond to his positive virtues, to those qualities that give him great 'presence' in the play — his generosity to friend and foe, his courage in the face of adversity and death, his outspoken leadership, his poetic way with words, above all an imperishable sense of honour which goes with him to the grave.

Though his eclipse is largely of his own making, our emotional impulse is to lay the blame on the other conspirators and to distance him, morally, from the lesser mortals of the play. Antony's tribute strikes a chord that we *want* to listen to:

> This was the noblest Roman of them all,
> All the conspirators save only he
> Did that they did in envy of great Caesar;

He only, in a general honest thought
And common good to all, made one of them.
His life was gentle, and the elements
So mixed in him, that Nature might stand up
And say to all the world, 'This was a man!'

(V.5.68–75)

The idealism of Brutus is certainly a mixed blessing — and arguably tarnished, by the stain of ambition. But he has died as he has lived, honourably. We respond to him, warts and all, as we respond to Shakespeare's other heroes. Shakespeare entitled his play 'The Tragedy of Julius Caesar'. But it is, first and foremost, the tragedy of Brutus.

AFTERTHOUGHTS

1

What further parallels could be identified between Brutus and Macbeth, other than those suggested by Campbell on pages 82 and 84?

2

What assumptions does Campbell make about Brutus's motives for joining the conspiracy (page 88)? Do you find the assumptions reasonable?

3

Do you agree that Brutus 'has died as he has lived, honourably' (page 89)?

4

Compare the argument of this essay with the essay by Cunningham (pages 28–37). Which viewpoint — if either — do you find more persuasive?

George Watson

*George Watson teaches in the English
Department at the University of
Aberdeen, and is the author of numerous
critical studies.*

ESSAY

The spirit of Caesar

In his 1949 New Cambridge edition of the play, John Dover
Wilson remarks that when Brutus exclaims 'We all stand up
against the spirit of Caesar':

> he sums up the play in one line. For the spirit of Caesar, which
> was the destiny of Rome, is the fate against which Brutus
> struggles in vain. And his failure to do so is his tragedy (and
> ours), inasmuch as Caesarism is a secular threat to the human
> spirit, and the living 'Julius', as Shakespeare shows him, is the
> mouthpiece of that threat.

Dover Wilson is surely correct to stress the thematic centrality
of Brutus's words. However, his interpretation of them as a
noble promulgation of anti-autocratic sentiment wholly en-
dorsed by Shakespeare is more contentious. Perhaps — given
the time at which the edition was prepared — Hitler and
Mussolini are too much in the editor's eyes. In fact, my argument is that Shakespeare shows that Brutus gets the distinction
between the body of the physical Julius and the spirit of Caesar
completely wrong, that he comprehensively misreads the political issues, and that he becomes lost in a moral miasma in that
grey area where politics and ethics intersect (which is every-
where, now as then).

The body and the spirit

We must begin with those famous words uttered by Brutus:

> We all stand up against the spirit of Caesar,
> And in the spirit of men there is no blood.
> O, that we then could come by Caesar's spirit,
> And not dismember Caesar! But, alas,
> Caesar must bleed for it.

(II.1.167–171)

Commentators have remarked the basic illogicality of Brutus's position here: if in the spirit of men there is no blood, then why should one assume that killing the body will also kill the spirit? Even if we accept the notion that 'political principles are not disembodied . . . but incarnate' (which seems to me highly dubious), Brutus, in his own rigid *distinction* of body and spirit which simultaneously *identifies* them, seems confused.

Can one destroy the spirit of Caesar by spilling his blood? This is not a literalist's inept question. Throughout the play, Shakespeare stresses the illogicality of Brutus's position by showing that there is no necessary correlation between the spirit and the frail body. In the very first scene, in fact, we are given what appears in retrospect to be an ironic gloss on Brutus's words. Mere death, physical dissolution, does not seem to have lessened the power of the spirit of Pompey over the allegiances of Flavius and Marullus. The scene suggests the pervasiveness of 'Caesarism' — and possibly its inevitability — in the Roman state, not just by showing us the monarchical sentiments of the Plebeians, but by emphasising that the Tribunes themselves, opponents of Caesar though they be, are thoroughly Caesarist in their attitudes to Pompey. The analogy is clear, if not hammered home: the spirit of Caesar may have as little connection with the physical Julius as the corpse of Pompey has with the still potent allure of his name. In short, the futility of the conspiracy is foreshadowed even before it has begun.

In Act I scene 2, Cassius reveals most strikingly his inability to understand how greatness and power can be compatible with physical infirmities:

> And this man
> Is now become a god, and Cassius is

A wretched creature, and must bend his body
If Caesar carelessly but nod on him.
He had a fever when he was in Spain,
And when the fit was on him, I did mark
How he did shake; 'tis true, this god did shake;
His coward lips did from their colour fly,
And that same eye whose bend doth awe the world
Did lose his lustre; I did hear him groan;
Ay, and that tongue of his, that bade the Romans
Mark him and write his speeches in their books,
'Alas!' it cried, 'Give me some drink, Titinius',
As a sick girl.

(I.2.115–128)

Cassius's bafflement here before the contradiction — as it seems
to him — of a Colossus who sneezes, serves in its very naïvety to
keep before us in an extremely vivid way the idea that the spirit
of Caesar and his body may not be identical. Shakespeare
further stresses the point in his presentation of the dictator
himself. In all his appearances both public and domestic we have
two figures: the great Caesar who is already half a god, a legend
in his own lifetime, the mighty emperor-to-be, in short the spirit
of Caesarism incarnate, and on the other hand, the human being
behind this marmoreal figure. It is this ordinary human with his
deafness and proneness to epilepsy who bleeds under the assassins' daggers. Shakespeare shows us that the spirit of Caesar,
against which Brutus and the others 'stand up', is almost a
separate identity, and much less vulnerable to those daggers.

Indeed, an idea central to the whole dramatic conception of
the play is that the spirit of Caesar is even more potent once the
man himself is dead. In Antony's powerful words (at III.1.270ff)
that spirit is seen as hungrily energetic, as kingly in spite of
Brutus, and as thirsting for vengeance:

And Caesar's spirit, ranging for revenge,
With Ate by his side, come hot from hell,
Shall in these confines with a monarch's voice
Cry havoc and let slip the dogs of war

Caesar's body is still warm when Brutus is first brought up
against the painful truth that his project — the destruction of
Caesarism — is doomed to futility. At the end of his speech in

the Forum, one of the Plebeians calls out in congratulation of Brutus 'Let him be Caesar' (III.2.51). This is hardly subtle, but is undeniably effective as oblique comment on Brutus's misguidedness. Indeed, Act III ends with a kind of grotesque parody of Brutus's attempt to destroy Caesar's spirit by killing his body, when we see the poet Cinna torn to pieces by the angry mob, simply because he bears the same name as one of the conspirators. As one of the crowd shouts, 'pluck but his name out of his heart, and turn him going' (III.3.34). Brutus has also tried — and failed — to pluck Caesar's name out of his heart.

The whole of the latter part of the play — Acts IV and V — might well be called 'Caesar's Revenge'. His spirit is pervasive (at one point even dramatically manifesting itself as a ghost), and ultimately triumphs completely over Brutus and Cassius. Both see themselves at the moment of death as overcome by Caesar rather than by the military skills of Antony and Octavius, and both address him directly:

> CASSIUS Caesar, thou art revenged
> Even with the sword that killed thee.
>
> (V.3.45)

> BRUTUS Caesar, now be still;
> I killed not thee with half so good a will.
>
> (V.5.51–52)

Brutus in particular has become aware of his terrible mistake in confusing body and spirit. He realises, eventually, that he could not 'come by' Caesar's spirit by dismembering him, that that spirit was not only invulnerable to crude physical assault but also capable of striking back:

> O Julius Caesar, thou art mighty yet!
> Thy spirit walks abroad, and turns our swords
> In our own proper entrails.
>
> (V.3.94–96)

To sum up, Shakespeare's persistent dissociation of Caesar's body and spirit gives a satisfying unity of conception to *Julius Caesar*, and helps to explain why the play is called that, and not *Marcus Brutus*. From the perspective of this guiding idea, we can see more clearly why Shakespeare is willing to take the risk (which a lesser dramatist might well have flinched from) of placing this most famous of political murders in the middle rather than at the climax of his action. Some commentators (such as E M Forster) have implied that *Julius Caesar* is an episodic play, that Shakespeare's imagination was only sporadically fired, in the scenes depicting the murder, the speeches in the Forum, and the quarrel, and for the rest somewhat dutifully versified a world-famous story. On the contrary, the master-notion of the power of Caesar's spirit, with all its attendant ironies, confirms the play as most tightly structured and coherent.

The murder: ritual or butchery?

As has frequently been pointed out, Brutus tries to turn Caesar's murder into a ritual sacrifice:

> Let's kill him boldly, but not wrathfully;
> Let's carve him as a dish fit for the gods,
> Not hew him as a carcass fit for hounds.

> (II.1.172–174)

It is Brutus too who suggests immediately after the deed that the conspirators stoop and bathe their hands in Caesar's blood, in a gesture obviously designed to try to sacramentalise the murder. (It is pertinent that Shakespeare invented these touches: they are not found in Plutarch.) There is no suggestion here that Brutus is an ogre besotted with gore; but just as he was wrong, as we have seen, about the spirit of Caesar, so is he mistaken about the moral and imaginative impact of Caesar's blood. From this moment until the end of the play, Shakespeare explores the connotations of the image he found in Plutarch, that Caesar 'was hacked and mangled among them, as a wild beast taken of hunters', a phrasing which suggests ideas very different from those suggested by Brutus's 'dish fit for the gods'. Antony rams home these differences almost immediately when, after shaking the bloody hands of the conspirators in a grimly ironic parody of the ceremonial hand-shaking which had taken place in Brutus's orchard (see II.1.112), he addresses Caesar's corpse:

> Here wast thou bayed, brave hart;

Here didst thou fall; and here thy hunters stand,
Signed in thy spoil, and crimsoned in thy lethe.

(III.1.204–206)

The hunting metaphors, probably suggested by Plutarch, cast an ironic light back on Brutus's fantasy of serving up a dish for the gods. When he is left alone, Antony can be even more explicit, calling the conspirators 'butchers' (III.1.255), and his showing of Caesar's much stained and torn mantle and his hacked body, in the Forum, has its powerful effect on us as well as on the Roman citizens. The murder of Caesar *is* in some sense what Brutus denies it to be, 'a savage spectacle' (III.1.223). The last extended account, late in the play, of Caesar's death comes again from Antony. With great intensity Antony reverts to the savage image of the final moments of a hunt when the hounds fawn upon their quarry before tearing it to pieces (he is alluding to the conspirators' flattery of Caesar, and to Brutus's Judas-like kiss):

You showed your teeth like apes, and fawned like hounds,
And bowed like bondmen, kissing Caesar's feet;
Whilst damnèd Casca, like a cur, behind
Struck Caesar on the neck.

(V.1.41–44)

The densely woven network of images of blood, animals and the hunt enforces on us the knowledge of how the slaying of Caesar obstinately refuses to become the ritual sacrifice of Brutus's imagination: the picture of the daggers 'hack[ing] one another in the sides of Caesar' (another phrase from Antony, V.1.40) is superimposed on Brutus's vision, and ultimately obliterates it.

Political consequences

The morality of the conspirators' action may be open to debate — it is, after all, possible to commit a wrong deed from the best of motives (Dover Wilson, for one, would not even agree that it *is* a wrong deed, since he sees more of the tyrant in Caesar than I can). There can be little argument, however about the appalling political consequences of their deed. Brutus lent himself to the conspiracy for the common good of Rome, in order to right the 'general wrong' as he puts it (III.1.170), to recall the city from its dangerous flirtation with absolutism to a renewed embrace of the republican virtues with which he identifies. The effects of the assassination are diametrically opposed to those he hoped for. Even if one accepts his view that Rome is groaning under the yoke of 'high-sighted tyranny' (II.1.118) which, if the evidence of the cheerful citizens of the first scene counts for anything, seems to be more than slightly exaggerated, there can hardly by any dispute that Rome after Caesar's death is worse off. 'Liberty, freedom and enfranchisement!' proclaims Cassius as Caesar's body slumps at the feet of Pompey's statue; what the play shows, however, is the terrible truth embodied in Antony's prophetic soliloquy at III.1.262ff.:

> A curse shall light upon the limbs of men;
> Domestic fury and fierce civil strife
> Shall cumber all the parts of Italy;
> Blood and destruction shall be so in use,
> And dreadful objects so familiar,
> That mothers shall but smile when they behold
> Their infants quartered with the hand of war . . .

This horrifying picture looks back to the prophecy of the Bishop of Carlisle in *Richard II* that 'the blood of English shall manure the ground' if Richard is deposed, and forward to the vivid descriptions of the sufferings of Scotland under Macbeth. In *Julius Caesar* it is not long before Antony's vision becomes reality, with the mob tearing the harmless Cinna to pieces (III.3). Even more chilling is the cold-blooded judicial purge instituted by the triumvirs (IV.1), the horror of which is heightened by Shakespeare's emphasis on a ruthlessness prepared to set aside family ties:

> OCTAVIUS   Your brother too must die; consent you, Lepidus?
> LEPIDUS   I do consent.
> OCTAVIUS   Prick him down, Antony.
> LEPIDUS   Upon condition Publius shall not live,
>   Who is your sister's son, Mark Antony.
> ANTONY   He shall not live. Look, with a spot I damn him.

(IV.1.2–6)

Hardly 'liberty, freedom and enfranchisement'; and the play's

closing scenes are full of images of the fierce civil strife prophesied by Antony, with hints of the coming power struggle between
him and the frigidly passionless Octavius, whom we, like
Shakespeare's audience, know will be the first in a long line of
emperors. Brutus has not only not achieved his political goal:
the evidence is comprehensive that, instead of benefiting his
country, he has done it incalculable harm.

The critical controversy

Ernest Schanzer in *The Problem Plays of Shakespeare* (1963,
p. 10) remarks that:

> *Julius Caesar* is one of Shakespeare's most controversial plays.
> Commentators have been quite unable to agree on who is its
> principal character or whether it has one; on whether it is a
> tragedy and if so, of what kind; on whether Shakespeare wants
> us to consider the assassination as damnable or praiseworthy;
> while of all the chief characters in the play contradictory inter-
> pretations have been given.

It is indeed important to stress the controversial nature of the
play. The argument put forward above, while I believe it to be
central and true, does not explain the effect of great complexity
Julius Caesar arouses in the minds of audiences and readers. To
oversimplify, while the presentation of 'the story' is clear-cut
and relatively straightforward, the presentation of the characters
is emotionally complex. Shakespeare draws on a long tradition
of debate and dispute about Caesar and the other figures in the
history to manipulate our sympathies vigorously for and against
each of them. The effect is to engage and involve us in the
drama in a very immediate way so that we are made to *experience*
its problems and complexities, to *feel* the tension between personal character and public action, the difficult necessity of distinguishing the image of Caesar (or of Brutus) from the mortal
Julius (or Marcus). *Julius Caesar* invites partisan responses
from us: it could not be less like a costume drama.

To put this in terms of a brief critical history of responses to
this most famous assassination, the majority of writers on the
subject from antiquity onwards would have agreed with the
reading offered above that the murder itself was a gross mistake
fraught with evil consequences. The Tudor disposition to see

history in terms of the deeds of princes, to believe in benevolent monarchy and to abhor civil war as the worst of evils (and an ever-present threat) can only have strengthened the generally shared condemnation of the actual murder of Caesar which would have been part of the pervasive ideology of Shakespeare's times. Thus the English translator of Appian's *Roman History* (1578) — a book Shakespeare seems to have known — saw in the fate of Caesar's murderers 'How God plagueth them that conspire againste theyr Prince' and considers the book to give 'an evident demonstration that peoples rule must give place and Princes power prevayle'. Another survey of 'the Continuall Factions, Tumults, and Massacres of the Romans' warns against 'complotting in darke conventicles against superiors'. Shakespeare does not view the murder in the crudely and emphatically moralistic way suggested by the tone of these quotations; but, as shown above, he presents it as at best foolish and self-defeating, at worst a 'savage spectacle'.

Whatever might have been thought about 'the story', however, one finds in nearly all the biographers and historians of Caesar and his contemporaries before 1599 divided responses to the chief personages around whom Shakespeare was to build his drama. (This is true of Plutarch himself, Shakespeare's main source.) Caesar was shown as brave, energetic, eloquent, and as a great and charismatic leader, but also as ruthless and unduly ambitious. Brutus was seen as noble in the disinterestedness of his republican and Stoic principles, yet also as the ungrateful killer of his benefactor, as a treacherous and foolish man. And so one could go on. This may suggest that the heart of the dramatic appeal of the play lies in the characters, though one cannot really separate character and action in this way. The story, however, was universally known and thus imposed its own constraints. What can be said with certainty is that Shakespeare elevates the tradition of conflicting response, which goes back to the first tellings of the Caesar story, into what may be called the major dramatic principle behind the treatment of the characters of *Julius Caesar*.

The presentation of Caesar

Thus, from the account of the play given so far, it might be thought that Caesar is purely and simply a great man struck down in a dastardly manner. But there is much evidence in the play of another side to Caesar. It could be argued that his initial appearances, on the feast of Lupercal, show him up in a most unflattering light as a kind of oriental despot surrounded by sycophants and servile yes-men. Thoughout, he frequently seems pompous and boastful:

> Danger knows full well
> That Caesar is more dangerous than he.
> We are two lions littered in one day.
> And I the elder and more terrible.

(II.2.44–47)

This pomposity is highlighted by its constant juxtaposition with all too human failings:

> I rather tell thee what is to be feared
> Than what I fear; for always I am Caesar.
> Come on my right hand, for this ear is deaf

(I.2.210–212)

Even when the failings are not physical, Caesar's claims to be without fear are totally undercut by the evidence of nervousness and vacillation in his domestic interlude with Calphurnia (II.2). If there is one feature which sums up the unappealing side of Caesar, it is that too often he attempts to set himself outside or above or beyond mere common humanity:

> I could be well moved, if I were as you;
> If I could pray to move, prayers would move me;
> But I am constant as the northern star,
> Of whose true-fixed and resting quality
> There is no fellow in the firmament.

(III.1.58–63)

Yet we must be careful not to read our own standards into the standards of cultures widely separated from us both in space and, even more importantly, in time. Indeed, one of the great values of reading the literature of the past is that it makes us aware of the relativity of our own values. For the Romans, the creation of a striking public image was a necessary part of public life. Like Machiavelli, many centuries later, they believed in the need for the ruler to be an actor, a dramatic figure, for him to be able to put on a show. The histrionic element in Roman public life is most interestingly attested to by Caesar's enemies, whose thoughts turn instantly to the theatre at the very crisis of their lives:

> CASSIUS How many ages hence
> Shall this our lofty scene be acted over,
> In states unborn, and accents yet unknown!
> BRUTUS How many times shall Caesar bleed in sport,
> That now on Pompey's basis lies along,
> No worthier than the dust!
>
> (III.1.111–116)

Further, in the Renaissance, self-regard, a proper concern for one's public image and reputation, was a high virtue, one of the pillars of society itself. (As late as 1841, Thomas Carlyle in *On Heroes, Hero-Worship and the Heroic in History* argued that religion and society were founded on hero-worship.) One need only think of the anguish of Cassio, in *Othello*, who considers his loss of reputation the loss of the immortal part of himself. Nowadays public figures are less capable of the do-it-yourself creation of the necessary image: they hire advertising agencies to do their 'boasting' for them.

None of this is to suggest that Caesar never boasts, or is modest; it is only to draw attention to cultural and temporal differences, which require modification of our judgements. At any rate, there is plenty of evidence of qualities in Caesar more immediately attractive than his high Roman standing on his own dignity. He clearly *does* have the power to command; but that goes along with nice — if calculated — moments of self-abnegation ('What touches us ourself shall be last served', he tells Artemidorus at III.1.8). His courtesy and hospitality come out most clearly — and ironically — in his greeting of the conspirators in II.2, where Shakespeare humanises the Colossus with superb touches like:

> Caius Ligarius,
> Caesar was ne'er so much your enemy
> As that same ague which hath made you lean.
>
> (II.2.111–113)

The concern here for the health of Caius Ligarius may suggest another aspect of the complex effect created by Shakespeare. Caesar's own physical infirmities, so much scorned by Cassius, and serving from one point of view to undercut Caesar's assertions of his freedom from humanity, may also tend to evoke our sympathy for him. Indeed, Cassius's argument may be turned on its head: when, in I.2, he tries to enforce on Brutus his own sense that it is ludicrous that a man who is physically inferior should 'bear the palm alone', we may well feel that his story of the swimming-contest serves only to epitomise the triumph of Caesar's spirit over his physical frailties. Finally, we should note that Caesar exists in this complex way not only in himself, but in the minds of others, and that in the very different views of him held by Cassius, Brutus and Antony our sense of that complexity is intensified.

Caesar and Brutus

If the play does nothing else, then, it shows us in its portrait of Caesar that great historical personages and issues are rarely understandable in simplistic terms. For Brutus, Caesar's death is justified by his tyranny. A hypothetical tyranny, we must say, since the play gives no evidence of it (save perhaps in the sinister phrase that informs us the Flavius and Marullus 'are put to silence', I.2.283). Brutus himself admits this (II.1.10–34); and Shakespeare departs from his source to stress that the people love Caesar. Still, when all the favourable evidence has been taken into account, we may still feel that Caesar is a man too much in the grip of an ideal conception of himself. As J I M Stewart puts it:

> the overwhelming, immediate and public Caesar is the creation of an inflexible will, is a rigid mask which has proved so potent that its creator himself can scarcely regard it but with awe
>
> (*Character and Motive in Shakespeare*, 1949, p. 53)

This is judicious, but if the invention of a rigid public mask be a fault in Caesar, may we not see the same process at work in Brutus?

There is a tendency in Brutus to see himself as a public embodiment of republican principle, a tendency cunningly played on by Cassius at I.2.157ff, where his references to Brutus's distinguished king-hating ancestors lead Brutus to mount his rhetorical high horse:

> Brutus had rather be a villager
> Than to repute himself a son of Rome
> Upon these hard conditions ...

(I.2.171–173)

(We might note that Brutus can be every bit as pompously rhetorical as Caesar, who is not the only person in the play to speak of himself in the third person.) His soliloquy at II.1.10–34 has an amazing theoretical abstractness about it, and it is hard not to feel that its convoluted logic is the product of a mind in the grip of an idealised self-conception — that Brutus is seeing himself as the latest and noblest in a long line of tyrant-killers. He too has his public role to live up to. 'Role' is the word — as we have already seen, he tries to turn the murder into symbolic theatre, and for his own part in it, he would 'bear it as our Roman actors do' (II.1.226). David Daiches sums him up well:

> He is a kind of hero, whose idealism and nobility and intelligence and kindness and generosity are curiously combined with his vanity and naïveté and love of abstractions and tendency to theatricalize himself. He is at his best as husband, friend, master, in domestic situations, and at his worst as patriot and public benefactor.
>
> (Shakespeare: Julius Caesar 1976, p. 56)

So, if there are two Caesars, there are also two Brutuses. Shakespeare shows that public life imposes its necessities and distortions on all those involved in it. In the case of Brutus, we are made aware that impersonal causes may betray the human heart into going against its own deeper impulses, that public generosity may issue in 'a savage spectacle'. The sense that for all their differences Brutus and Caesar in a deeper way are reflections of each other does something more: it communicates that idea of similarity in dissimilarity which Coleridge considered one of the most profound pleasures that art has to offer.

Continuing relevance

At the beginning of this essay, I rebuked Dover Wilson for

reading *Julius Caesar* too readily by the light of the most recent European experience of dictatorship; and clearly, we must attend to what is in the play rather than write our own. However, at least Dover Wilson is responding in the right *kind* of way. Even if it were possible to read *Julius Caesar* entirely through Roman and/or Renaissance spectacles, to break free of our inevitable conditioning by our own twentieth-century context (and we must of course be aware of the relativity of our values), it would be a mistake to try to turn the play reductively into merely a monument to dead ideas. It is burningly relevant. It asks us to consider the perennial questions. Does the end justify the means? (think of that acronymic trio who so affect our world, the IRA, the PLO, the ANC, all those 'hearts with one purpose alone', as Yeats put it in 'Easter 1916'). Can issues ever be divorced from personalities? (think of Mrs Thatcher and 'Thatcherism'). Can an idea ever be 'stopped' by 'stopping' the person in whom it is embodied?

'The spirit of Caesar' was our theme, and to end with an illustration of the continuing relevance of Shakespeare's concept to our own times, I would cite the executions of Pearse, MacDonagh and the other leaders of the Easter Rising of 1916 in Ireland. The men were shot, but in death what they stood for became paradoxically more potent. Their ideal was not Caesar's, but their spirit, like his on Rome, continues to exercise its influence, for good or ill, on Ireland to the present day. As W B Yeats, another great poet, understood, the most powerful rule of all may be the rule of the dead:

> You say that we should still the land
> Till Germany's overcome;
> But who is there to argue that
> Now Pearse is deaf and dumb?
> And is their logic to outweigh
> MacDonagh's bony thumb?

('Sixteen Dead Men')

Long ago, Shakespeare knew the weight of Caesar's bony thumb.

AFTERTHOUGHTS

What do you understand by Watson's claim that the Tribunes 'are thoroughly Caesarist in their attitudes to Pompey' (page 92)?

What alternative title to Acts IV and V could you suggest, other than 'Caesar's Revenge' (page 94)?

Do you agree that the killing of Caesar is 'a wrong deed' (page 96) — and, if so, on what grounds?

What 'similarity in dissimilarity' (page 103) does Watson identify between Caesar and Brutus in this essay?

Richard Wilson

Richard Wilson is Lecturer in English at Lancaster University, and the author of numerous critical studies.

ESSAY

Drama as pretext: plot and pattern in *Julius Caesar*

Julius Caesar was the first Shakespearean play we know to have been acted at the Globe and was perhaps performed for the opening of the new Bankside playhouse in 1599. The Swiss tourist Thomas Platter saw it on 21 September, and his impressions locate the work within the different cultural practices that went to make the Elizabethan playhouse. To our minds, accustomed to a decorous image of both Shakespeare and ancient Rome, it is just this collision of codes and voices which makes the traveller's report seem so bizarre and jarring:

> After lunch, at about two o'clock, I and my party crossed the river, and there in the house with the thatched roof we saw an excellent performance of the tragedy of the first emperor, Julius Caesar, with about fifteen characters; and after the play, according to their custom, they did a most elegant and curious dance, two dressed in men's clothes and two in women's[1]

---

[1] T S Dorsch, ed., The Arden Shakespeare: *Julius Caesar* (London, 1955), p. vii.

Along with the scarves, doublets and hose of Shakespeare's Romans, we can absorb the cultural shock of 'the house with the thatched roof', but the elegant jig of Caesar and the boy dressed as Caesar's wife is too alienating a mixture for us of the 'merry and tragical'. Even the Swiss tourist thought it a curious local custom, and he was lucky to see it, because by 1612 'all Jigs, Rhymes and Dances after Plays' had been 'utterly abolished', to prevent the 'tumults and outrages whereby His Majesty's peace is often broke', alleged to be caused by the 'cut-purses and other lewd and ill-disposed persons' who were attracted by them into the auditorium in droves at the close of each performance.[2] Platter was an observer of a theatre already expelling gate-crashers and purging itself of the popular customs that had legtimised their unwelcome intrusion. He was witnessing what Francis Barker has described as 'the seeds of naturalism' growing up inside the Elizabethan theatre, where clowns would learn to 'speak no more than is set down for them', and laughter — as Hamlet prescribes — would be conditional on the 'necessary question of the play'. Authority in this theatre would come to be concentrated in what Hamlet proprietorially tells the players are 'my lines' (III.2.1–45), and the mastery of the author as producer would be founded on the suppression of just those practices which Platter found so picturesque and noteworthy: the unwritten scenario of the mummers' dance, transvestite mockery, Dick Tarlton's 'villainous' comic improvisation, and the raucous collective gesture of hearty disrespect for 'His Majesty's peace'. Elite and popular traditions coexist in embarrassed tension in the entry from Platter's travel diary, where the excellence of the classical tragedy consorts so oddly with the curiosity of the antic dance. The diarist did not realise, of course, that the sequence he recorded represented the division between two cultures and was for one of them the literal final fling, nor that 'the house with the thatched roof' was the scene, even as he applauded the performance, of bitter social separation.[3]

The opening words of *Julius Caesar* seem to know themselves, nevertheless, as a declaration of company policy towards

---

[2] E K Chambers, *The Elizabethan Stage* (Oxford, Oxford University Press, 1923), IV: pp 340–341 (Order of the Middlesex Sessions, October 1 1612).

[3] F Barker, *The Tremulous Private Body: essays in subjection* (London, 1984), p. 18.

the new theatre's audience. They are a rebuke to the temerity of the commoners for daring to enter the vicinity: 'home, you idle creatures, get you home:/ Is this a holiday?' Dressed in their festive 'best apparel', these 'mechanical' men have mistaken the occasion for a 'holiday', and to the rhetorical question 'Is this a holiday?' they are now given the firm answer that for them, at least, it is an ordinary 'labouring day' (I.1.4). This is an encounter, then, that situates what follows explicitly within the contemporary debate about the value or 'idleness' of popular culture, a debate in which, as Hill has written, 'two modes of life, with their different needs and standards, are in conflict, as England moves out of the agricultural Middle Ages into the modern industrial world'.[4] And as Flavius and his colleague Marullus order the Plebeians back to work, it is a confrontation that confirms Hill's thesis that the Puritan attack on popular festivity was a strategy to control the emerging manufacturing workforce. The Tribunes oppose 'holiday' because it blurs distinctions between labour and reward, and the deserving poor and the shiftless work-shy, just as their counterparts the London Aldermen complained that the playhouses lured 'the prentices and servants of the City from their works'. In fact, the Tribunes' speeches echo *The Anatomy of Abuses* of 1583 by the merchants' censor Philip Stubbes, and in so doing the actors of the Globe were disarming one of the most powerful, because pragmatic, objections to their trade. As Thomas Nashe protested when the first playhouse was erected on the South Bank of the Thames in 1592, professional players were not to be confused with 'squirting bawdy comedians'; they were distinct from 'the pantaloon, whore and zany' of the market-place. Their preferred patrons were 'Gentlemen of the Court, and the Inns of Court, and captains and soldiers' (a clientele corroborated by the 1602 police-raid on the brothels and playhouses), and the citizens could rest assured that 'they heartily wish they might be troubled with none of their youth nor their prentices'. So theatre-impresarios such as Philip Henslowe were careful to obey the ban on 'interludes and plays on the Sabbath', closing their doors on city workers (as James I complained) on the only afternoon when they were

---

[4] C Hill, *Society and Puritanism in Pre-Revolutionary England* (Harmondsworth, 1986), p. 163.

officially free. If working men were present to hear the beginning of *Julius Caesar* and stayed despite it, the implication was clear that they had no business to be there. Theatre, it had to be inferred, was now itself a legitimate business with no room for the 'idle'.[5]

The first scene acted at the Globe can be interpreted, then, as a manoeuvre in the campaign to legitimise the Shakespearean stage and to market it as segregated from the riotousness of London's artisanal culture. As historians such as Peter Burke have demonstrated, revelry and rebellion were entangled in Renaissance popular entertainments, and it was no coincidence that insurrections such as the Peasants' Revolts of 1381 and 1450, the Evil May Day riot of 1517, or Kett's Rebellion of 1549 should have been sparked off at seasonal plays or have had vivid carnivalesque features. A function of folk drama had been to cement the ties and obligations of an agrarian community, and when these were threatened in the transition to capitalist social relations, it was through the 'rough music' of folk customs — mummings, wakes and *charivaris* — that the new masters were called to ritual account. The world of carnival, with its travesty and inversion, was a standing *pretext* for protest; but if, as happened increasingly in early modern Europe, rulers chose to ignore the 'wild justice' of festivity, there could be what Burke calls a violent 'switching of codes, from the language of ritual to the language of rebellion', when 'the wine barrel blew its top'.[6] This is what happened spectacularly in the bloody carnival at the French town of Romans in 1580, and it was what happened less explosively in London during the crisis years of the 1590s, when hunger and unemployment drove 'disordered people of the common sort' (in the Aldermanic phrase) 'to assemble themselves and make matches for their lewd ungodly practices' at Shrovetide, May Day or Midsummer; festivals when, like the workers in *Julius Caesar*, they could still 'cull out a holiday' from the industrial week (I.1.49). Lumping all revels with re-

---

[5] T Nashe, *Pierce Penniless* in *The Unfortunate Traveller and other Works*, ed. J B Steane (Harmondsworth, 1972), pp. 114–115; E K Chambers, *The Elizabethan Stage* (Oxford, 1923), IV, p. 307; L A Govett, ed., *The King's Book of Sports* (London, 1890), p. 30.
[6] P Burke, *Popular Culture in Early Modern Europe* (London, 1978), p. 203.

bellion, the authorities were instinctively sure that riotous 'apprentices and servants drew their infection' from the play-houses, where people also caught the plague; but, as Nashe insisted, this analogy was a kind of category mistake which miscalculated the new theatres' ideological role. If the playhouse was, as coroners reported, the site of 'frays and bloodshed', it was as the target of violence, not the origin, as when apprentices rampaged on Shrove Tuesday each year and 'put playhouses to the sack and bawdyhouses to the spoil' (in 1617 wrecking the Cockpit Theatre with the loss of several lives). The rough music of *charivari* was hollered in anger from outside the walls of Shakespeare's Globe.

'The disorders of the 1590s were the most serious to menace the metropolis in the decades up to the Civil War', the urban historian Peter Clark concludes, and what concerns him is how this unprecedented metropolitan crisis was managed and con-tained.[7] The answer must lie at least partly in the success with which the language of carnival as a discourse of legitimation was commandeered by the professional players during these years and then tamed. For as texts like *Julius Caesar* remind us, and as history, in Foucault's words, 'constantly teaches us, discourse is not simply that which translates struggles or sys-tems of domination, but is the thing for which struggle takes place'.[8] It was no mere evasion of authority, therefore, which led to Shakespeare's theatre being resituated on the criminalised southern bank of the Thames, where Platter and his party rowed to unbrace and recreate themselves after lunch. In the complex zoning of the city that dates precisely from this time, Southwark was to occupy the position of a policed and cordoned annexe to the business and residential districts on the city's northern side, such as wealthy Bishopsgate, where the playwright resided. Within its commercialised liberties, the Bankside was to have the status of a permanent but strictly circumscribed carnival in the city's economy of repression and indulgence, a disposal-valve in its regulation of productivity and waste. Shady and sinister,

---

[7] P Clarke, *The European Crisis of the 1590s: essays in comparitive history* (London, 1985), p. 54.

[8] M Foucault, 'The Order of Discourse', trans. I McLeod, in R Young, ed., *Untying the Text: A Post-Structuralist Reader* (London, 1981), pp. 52–53.

until the final suppression of Hogarth's Southwark Fair in 1762, the South Bank was to function as the unconscious of the capital of trade. Nor, in this topography of desire, was it accidental that the Globe was built beside those very institutions that, in Foucault's analysis, shaped the discourses of modern subjectivity, Ringed by reconstructed prisons such as the Marshalsea and the Clink, and flanked by the newly refounded St Thomas's Hospital, the playhouse meshed with a chain of buildings charged with separating society from its unacceptable elements, whether the sick, the mad, the aged, the criminal, the bankrupt or the unemployed. The wooden operating theatre of St Thomas's survives as the celebrated arena where the early modern body was cut into its diseased and healthy parts. The 'Wooden O' of the Globe next door, which must have resembled it in design so much, operated in analogous ways upon the body politic to divide and control the visceral language of carnival, separating out productive revelry (or art) from the idleness and infection of rebellion.

If Thomas Platter was a naïve theatre critic, as a sociologist he was shrewder. 'England', he observed, 'is the servants' prison, because their masters and mistresses are so severe'. The foreign visitor could see what has been confirmed in detail by Lee Beier in his survey of masterless men and the vagrancy problem in Shakespearean England, that the public order system which Foucault dated from the founding of the Paris General Hospital in 1656 was already established in London by 1599.[9] It was a system based, however, less on crude severity than on the strategy of self-regimentation and surveillance which Brutus proposes in *Julius Caesar*, when he argues for a controlled and strictly rational rebellion:

> And let our hearts, as subtle masters do,
> Stir up their servants to an act of rage,
> And after seem to chide 'em. This shall make
> Our purpose necessary, and not envious
>
> (II.2.175–178)

---

[9] A L Beier, *Masterless Men: The vagrancy problem in England*, 1560–1640 (London, 1985), p. 164.

The Shakespearean text belongs to a historical moment when a bourgeois politics has not naturalised its own violence, and Brutus's *realpolitik* is a candid prospectus for the technique whereby modern authority produces subversion in both the society and individual to legitimise the order that subjects it. The Tribunes had relied on the ideological apparatus of religion to coerce the Plebeians, ordering them to 'fall upon [their] knees' and 'Pray to the gods' in contrition (I.1.53–54); but this philosophers' republic is more modern. Unruly passions and apprentices are both checked in such a regime, as Hal similarly operates as *agent provocateur* among the outcasts of Eastcheap, to make them 'known and hated' (*Henry IV, Part 2*, IV.4.73). This is a system of discipline whose subtlety, as Brutus recognises, depends not on how it obstructs, but on how it produces desire, which will no longer be so much forbidden, as the very ground through which subjection is constructed. And it is just this 'calculated, subtle technology of subjection', as analysed by Foucault, operating in the new factories, hospitals and schools of Elizabethan London, which explains why Mikhail Bakhtin has so little to say about either Shakespeare or England in his account of the subversiveness of carnival and laughter. His ideas have been applied to Elizabethan drama by critics such as Michael Bristol, who describe the 'carnivalisation' of Shakespearean literature by customary culture. The argument is not convincing because, as Umberto Eco has remarked, what Bakhtinians crucially forget in their idealisation of the people's carnival is precisely the revenge of Lent: the confinement of desire, that is to say, within a dialectic of transgression and containment. If carnival were always so emancipatory, Eco retorts, 'it would be impossible to explain why power uses circuses'.[10]

The material conditions of modern subjectivity are inscribed within the Shakespearean text. Thus, when Portia tries to persuade her husband to share the secret of the plot, she challenges him: 'Dwell I but in the suburbs/ Of your good pleasure? If it be

---

[10] M Foucault, *Discipline and Punish: The birth of the prison*, trans. A Sheridan (Harmondsworth, 1979). p. 221; U Eco, 'The Frames of Comic Freedom', in T Sebeok, ed., *Carnival!* (New York, 1984), p. 3; M Bakhtin, *Rabelais and his World*, trans. H Iswolsky (Bloomington, 1984), *passim*.

no more,/ Portia is Brutus' harlot' (II.2.268–306). Body and language are policed like London in a bourgeois family, but when Brutus succumbs to Portia's blackmail he destroys himself by failing to quarantine desire in the suburbs of the body, where it should have been confined, like the brothels on Bankside. Brutus learns 'How hard it is for women to keep counsel' when his 'enterprise' is divulged to his servant (II.4.9, 41), and is 'discovered' to give Antony forewarning (III.1, 13–20). In *Julius Caesar*, carnival — the language of the flesh — is a discourse that is mastered by the vigilant. Thus, the opening scenes take place on the feast of Lupercal: 14 February, St Valentine's Day and the approximate date of Mardi Gras. So Caesar's boisterous artisans connect with those 'bands of prentices, 3,000 or 4,000 strong, who on Shrove Tuesday do outrages in all directions, especially in the suburbs', in contemporary reports. In 1660 it would be these 'football' clubs that would man the barricades against the commonwealth at Shrovetide; and in the play they are recruited by Caesar to guard his coronation, when Antony runs in the race and he himself clowns in the Shroving game by pretending to give the 'rabblement' the freedom it shouts for. This would be the tactic of King James's *Book of Sports* (1618) and of royalist propagandists such as Herrick, when contrary to Bakhtin's thesis, the customs of 'May-poles, Hock-carts, Wassails, and Wakes' would be harnessed to social reaction. It belongs to the world of what Hill calls 'synthetic monarchy', of Henry VIII's May games and Elizabeth's Accession Day. For by appropriating festival Caesar turns politics into theatre, as the 'tag-rag people ... clap him and hiss him, according as he pleased and displeased them, as they do the players' (I.2.256–258). He is their Carnival King, a Lord of Misrule who governs by exploiting popular desires with his 'foolery' (I.2.234), manipulating 'fat,/ Sleek-headed men' (I.2.191–192), as he eggs Antony to revel 'long a-nights' with plays and music (II.2.116). Provoking them to 'sports, wildness, and much company' (II.1.189), Caesar is the master of revels who knows 'danger' belongs to the 'lean and hungry' who can discipline the body to their purposes. So, his Roman carnival becomes a model of authoritarian populism, the true regimen of bread and circuses.

AFTERTHOUGHTS

1

How helpful do you find records or reports of contemporary stagings of Shakespeare's plays?

2

What significance does Wilson attach in this essay to the play's opening scene (pages 107–109)?

3

What do you understand by 'category mistake' (page 110)?

4

Trace the arguments that lead to this essay's conclusion that 'Roman carnival becomes a model of authoritarian populism' (page 113).

INTRODUCTION

First, a word of warning. Good essays are the product of a creative engagement with literature. So never try to restrict your studies to what you think will be 'useful in the exam'. Ironically, you will restrict your grade potential if you do.

This doesn't mean, of course, that you should ignore the basic skills of essay writing. When you read critics, make a conscious effort to notice *how* they communicate their ideas. The guidelines that follow offer advice of a more explicit kind. But they are no substitute for practical experience. It is never easy to express ideas with clarity and precision. But the more often you tackle the problems involved and experiment to find your own voice, the more fluent you will become. So practise writing essays as often as possible.

HOW TO PLAN
AN ESSAY

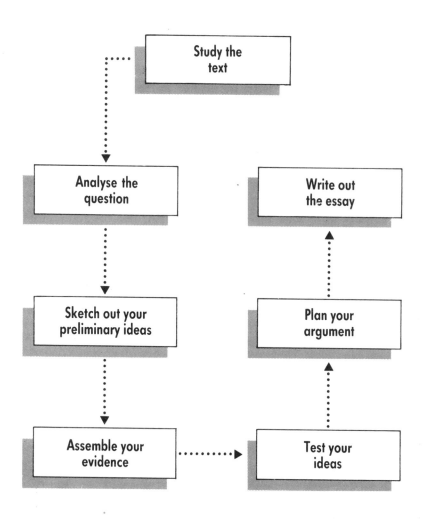

Study the text

The first step in writing a good essay is to get to know the set text well. Never write about a text until you are fully familiar with it. Even a discussion of the opening chapter of a novel, for example, should be informed by an understanding of the book as a whole. Literary texts, however, are by their very nature complex and on a first reading you are bound to miss many significant features. Re-read the book with care, if possible more than once. Look up any unfamiliar words in a good dictionary and if the text you are studying was written more than a few decades ago, consult the *Oxford English Dictionary* to find out whether the meanings of any terms have shifted in the intervening period.

Good books are difficult to put down when you first read them. But a more leisurely second or third reading gives you the opportunity to make notes on those features you find significant. An index of characters and events is often useful, particularly when studying novels with a complex plot or time scheme. The main aim, however, should be to record your *responses* to the text. By all means note, for example, striking images. But be sure to add *why* you think them striking. Similarly, record any thoughts you may have on interesting comparisons with other texts, puzzling points of characterisation, even what you take to be aesthetic blemishes. The important thing is to annotate fully and adventurously. The most seemingly idiosyncratic comment may later lead to a crucial area of discussion which you would otherwise have overlooked. It helps to have a working copy of the text in which to mark up key passages and jot down marginal comments (although obviously these practices are taboo when working with library, borrowed or valuable copies!). But keep a fuller set of notes as well and organise these under appropriate headings.

Literature does not exist in an aesthetic vacuum, however, and you should try to find out as much as possible about the context of its production and reception. It is particularly important to read other works by the same author and writings by contemporaries. At this early stage, you may want to restrict your secondary reading to those standard reference works, such as biographies, which are widely available in public libraries. In the long run, however, it pays to read as wide a range of critical studies as possible.

Some students, and tutors, worry that such studies may stifle the development of any truly personal response. But this won't happen if you are alert to the danger and read critically. After all, you wouldn't passively accept what a stranger told you in conversation. The fact that a critic's views are in print does not necessarily make them any more authoritative (as a glance at the review pages of the *TLS* and *London Review of Books* will reveal). So question the views you find: 'Does this critic's interpretation agree with mine and where do we part company?' 'Can it be right to try and restrict this text's meanings to those found by its author or first audience?' 'Doesn't this passage treat a theatrical text as though it were a novel?' Often it is views which you reject which prove most valuable since they challenge you to articulate your own position with greater clarity. Be sure to keep careful notes on what the critic wrote, and your *reactions* to what the critic wrote.

Analyse the question

You cannot begin to answer a question until you understand what task it is you have been asked to perform. Recast the question in your own words and reconstruct the line of reasoning which lies behind it. Where there is a choice of topics, try to choose the one for which you are best prepared. It would, for example, be unwise to tackle 'How far do you agree that in *Paradise Lost* Milton transformed the epic models he inherited from ancient Greece and Rome?' without a working knowledge of Homer and Virgil (or *Paradise Lost* for that matter!). If you do not already know the works of these authors, the question should spur you on to read more widely — or discourage you from attempting it at all. The scope of an essay, however, is not always so obvious and you must remain alert to the implied demands of each question. How could you possibly 'Consider the view that *Wuthering Heights* transcends the conventions of the Gothic novel' without reference to at least some of those works which, the question suggests, have *not* transcended Gothic conventions?

When you have decided on a topic, analyse the terms of the question itself. Sometimes these self-evidently require careful definition: *tragedy* and *irony*, for example, are notoriously difficult concepts to pin down and you will probably need to consult a good dictionary of literary terms. Don't ignore, however, those seemingly innocuous phrases which often smuggle in significant assumptions. 'Does Macbeth lack the nobility of the true tragic hero?' obviously invites you to discuss nobility and the nature of the tragic hero. But what of 'lack' and 'true' — do they suggest that the play would be improved had Shakespeare depicted Macbeth in a different manner? or that tragedy is superior to other forms of drama? Remember that you are not expected meekly to agree with the assumptions implicit in the question. Some questions are deliberately provocative in order to stimulate an engaged response. Don't be afraid to take up the challenge.

Sketch out your preliminary ideas

'Which comes first, the evidence or the answer?' is one of those chicken and egg questions. How can you form a view without inspecting the evidence? But how can you know which evidence is relevant without some idea of what it is you are looking for? In practice the mind reviews evidence and formulates preliminary theories or hypotheses at one and the same time, although for the sake of clarity we have separated out the processes. Remember that these early ideas are only there to get you started. You *expect* to modify them in the light of the evidence you uncover. Your initial hypothesis may be an instinctive 'gut-reaction'. Or you may find that you prefer to 'sleep on the problem', allowing ideas to gell over a period of time. Don't worry in either case. The mind is quite capable of processing a vast amount of accumulated evidence, the product of previous reading and thought, and reaching sophisticated intuitive judgements. Eventually, however, you are going to have to think carefully through any ideas you arrive at by such intuitive processes. Are they logical? Do they take account of all the relevant factors? Do they fully answer the question set? Are there any obvious reasons to qualify or abandon them?

Assemble your evidence

Now is the time to return to the text and re-read it with the question and your working hypothesis firmly in mind. Many of the notes you have already made are likely to be useful, but assess the precise relevance of this material and make notes on any new evidence you discover. The important thing is to cast your net widely and take into account points which tend to undermine your case as well as those that support it. As always, ensure that your notes are full, accurate, and reflect your own critical judgements.

You may well need to go outside the text if you are to do full justice to the question. If you think that the 'Oedipus complex' may be relevant to an answer on *Hamlet* then read Freud and a balanced selection of those critics who have discussed the appropriateness of applying psychoanalytical theories to the interpretation of literature. Their views can most easily be tracked down by consulting the annotated bibliographies held by most major libraries (and don't be afraid to ask a librarian for help in finding and using these). Remember that you go to works of criticism not only to obtain information but to stimulate you into clarifying your own position. And that since life is short and many critical studies are long, judicious use of a book's index and/or contents list is not to be scorned. You can save yourself a great deal of future labour if you carefully record full bibliographic details at this stage.

Once you have collected the evidence, organise it coherently. Sort the detailed points into related groups and identify the quotations which support these. You must also assess the relative importance of each point, for in an essay of limited length it is essential to establish a firm set of priorities, exploring some ideas in depth while discarding or subordinating others.

Test your ideas

As we stressed earlier, a hypothesis is only a proposal, and one that you fully expect to modify. Review it with the evidence before you. Do you really still believe in it? It would be surprising if you did not want to modify it in some way. If you cannot see any problems, others may. Try discussing your ideas with friends and relatives. Raise them in class discussions. Your tutor is certain to welcome your initiative. The critical process is essentially collaborative and there is absolutely no reason why you should not listen to and benefit from the views of others. Similarly, you should feel free to test your ideas against the theories put forward in academic journals and books. But do not just borrow what you find. Critically analyse the views on offer and, where appropriate, integrate them into your own pattern of thought. You must, of course, give full acknowledgement to the sources of such views.

Do not despair if you find you have to abandon or modify significantly your initial position. The fact that you are prepared to do so is a mark of intellectual integrity. Dogmatism is never an academic virtue and many of the best essays explore the *process* of scholarly enquiry rather than simply record its results.

Plan your argument

Once you have more or less decided on your attitude to the question (for an answer is never really 'finalised') you have to present your case in the most persuasive manner. In order to do this you must avoid meandering from point to point and instead produce an organised argument — a structured flow of ideas and supporting evidence, leading logically to a conclusion which fully answers the question. Never begin to write until you have produced an outline of your argument.

You may find it easiest to begin by sketching out its main stage as a flow chart or some other form of visual presentation. But eventually you should produce a list of paragraph topics. The paragraph is the conventional written demarcation for a unit of thought and you can outline an argument quite simply by briefly summarising the substance of each paragraph and then checking that these points (you may remember your English teacher referring to them as topic sentences) really do follow a coherent order. Later you will be able to elaborate on each topic, illustrating and qualifying it as you go along. But you will find this far easier to do if you possess from the outset a clear map of where you are heading.

All questions require some form of an argument. Even so-called 'descriptive' questions *imply* the need for an argument. An adequate answer to the request to 'Outline the role of Iago in *Othello*' would do far more than simply list his appearances on stage. It would at the very least attempt to provide some *explanation* for his actions — is he, for example, a representative stage 'Machiavel'? an example of pure evil, 'motiveless malignity'? or a realistic study of a tormented personality reacting to identifiable social and psychological pressures?

Your conclusion ought to address the terms of the question. It may seem obvious, but 'how far do you agree', 'evaluate', 'consider', 'discuss', etc, are *not* interchangeable formulas and your conclusion must take account of the precise wording of the question. If asked 'How far do you agree?', the concluding paragraph of your essay really should state whether you are in complete agreement, total disagreement, or, more likely, partial agreement. Each preceding paragraph should have a clear justification for its existence and help to clarify the reasoning which underlies your conclusion. If you find that a paragraph serves no good purpose (perhaps merely summarising the plot), do not hesitate to discard it.

The arrangement of the paragraphs, the overall strategy of the argument, can vary. One possible pattern is dialectical: present the arguments in favour of one point of view (**thesis**); then turn to counter-arguments or to a rival interpretation (**antithesis**); finally evaluate the competing claims and arrive at your own conclusion (**synthesis**). You may, on the other hand, feel so convinced of the merits of one particular case that you wish to devote your entire essay to arguing that viewpoint persuasively (although it is always desirable to indicate, however briefly, that you are aware of alternative, if flawed, positions). As the essays contained in this volume demonstrate, there are many other possible strategies. Try to adopt the one which will most comfortably accommodate the demands of the question and allow you to express your thoughts with the greatest possible clarity.

Be careful, however, not to apply abstract formulas in a mechanical manner. It is true that you should be careful to define your terms. It is *not* true that every essay should begin with 'The dictionary defines *x* as . . .'. In fact, definitions are often best left until an appropriate moment for their introduction arrives. Similarly every essay should have a beginning, middle and end. But it does not follow that in your opening paragraph you should announce an intention to write an essay, or that in your concluding paragraph you need to signal an imminent desire to put down your pen. The old adages are often useful reminders of what constitutes good practice, but they must be interpreted intelligently.

Write out the essay

Once you have developed a coherent argument you should aim to communicate it in the most effective manner possible. Make certain you clearly identify yourself, and the question you are answering. Ideally, type your answer, or at least ensure your handwriting is legible and that you leave sufficient space for your tutor's comments. Careless presentation merely distracts from the force of your argument. Errors of grammar, syntax and spelling are far more serious. At best they are an irritating blemish, particularly in the work of a student who should be sensitive to the nuances of language. At worst, they seriously confuse the sense of your argument. If you are aware that you have stylistic problems of this kind, ask your tutor for advice at the earliest opportunity. Everyone, however, is liable to commit the occasional howler. The only remedy is to give yourself plenty of time in which to proof-read your manuscript (often reading it aloud is helpful) before submitting it.

Language, however, is not only an instrument of communication; it is also an instrument of thought. If you want to think clearly and precisely you should strive for a clear, precise prose style. Keep your sentences short and direct. Use modern, straightforward English wherever possible. Avoid repetition, clichés and wordiness. Beware of generalisations, simplifications, and overstatements. Orwell analysed the relationship between stylistic vice and muddled thought in his essay 'Politics and the English Language' (1946) — it remains essential reading (and is still readily available in volume 4 of the Penguin *Collected Essays, Journalism and Letters*). Generalisations, for example, are always dangerous. They are rarely true and tend to suppress the individuality of the texts in question. A remark such as 'Keats always employs sensuous language in his poetry' is not only fatuous (what, after all, does it mean? is *every* word he wrote equally 'sensuous'?) but tends to obscure interesting distinctions which could otherwise be made between, say, the descriptions in the 'Ode on a Grecian Urn' and those in 'To Autumn'.

The intelligent use of quotations can help you make your points with greater clarity. Don't sprinkle them throughout your essay without good reason. There is no need, for example, to use them to support uncontentious statements of fact. 'Macbeth murdered Duncan' does not require textual evidence (unless you wish to dispute Thurber's brilliant parody, 'The Great Macbeth Murder Mystery', which reveals Lady Macbeth's father as the culprit!). Quotations should be included, however, when they are necessary to support your case. The proposition that Macbeth's imaginative powers wither after he has killed his king would certainly require extensive quotation: you would almost certainly want to analyse key passages from both before and after the murder (perhaps his first and last soliloquies?). The key word here is 'analyse'. Quotations cannot make your points on their own. It is up to you to demonstrate their relevance and clearly explain to your readers *why* you want them to focus on the passage you have selected.

Most of the academic conventions which govern the presentation of essays are set out briefly in the style sheet below. The question of gender, however, requires fuller discussion. More than half the population of the world is female. Yet many writers still refer to an undifferentiated *man*kind. Or write of the author and *his* public. We do not think that this convention has much to recommend it. At the very least, it runs the risk of introducing unintended sexist attitudes. And at times leads to such patent absurdities as 'Cleopatra's final speech asserts *man*'s true nobility'. With a little thought, you can normally find ways of expressing yourself which do not suggest that the typical author, critic or reader is male. Often you can simply use plural forms, which is probably a more elegant solution than relying on such awkward formulations as 's/he' or 'he and she'. You should also try to avoid distinguishing between male and female authors on the basis of forenames. Why *Jane* Austen and not *George* Byron? Refer to all authors by their last names unless there is some good reason not to. Where there may otherwise be confusion, say between TS and George Eliot, give the name in full when if first occurs and thereafter use the last name only.

Finally, keep your audience firmly in mind. Tutors and examiners are interested in understanding your conclusions and the processes by which you arrived at them. They are not interested in reading a potted version of a book they already know. **So don't pad out your work with plot summary.**

Hints for examinations

In an examination you should go through exactly the same processes as you would for the preparation of a term essay. The only difference lies in the fact that some of the stages will have had to take place before you enter the examination room. This should not bother you unduly. Examiners are bound to avoid the merely eccentric when they come to formulate papers and if you have read widely and thought deeply about the central issues raised by your set texts you can be confident you will have sufficient material to answer the majority of questions sensibly.

The fact that examinations impose strict time limits makes it *more* rather than less, important that you plan carefully. There really is no point in floundering into an answer without any idea of where you are going, particularly when there will not be time to recover from the initial error.

Before you begin to answer any question at all, study the entire paper with care. Check that you understand the rubric and know how many questions you have to answer and whether any are compulsory. It may be comforting to spot a title you feel confident of answering well, but don't rush to tackle it: read *all* the questions before deciding which *combination* will allow you to display your abilities to the fullest advantage. Once you have made your choice, analyse each question, sketch out your ideas, assemble the evidence, review your initial hypothesis, plan your argument, *before* trying to write out an answer. And make notes at each stage: not only will these help you arrive at a sensible conclusion, but examiners are impressed by evidence of careful thought.

Plan your time as well as your answers. If you have practised writing timed essays as part of your revision, you should not find this too difficult. There can be a temptation to allocate extra time to the questions you know you can answer well; but this is always a short-sighted policy. You will find yourself left to face a question which would in any event have given you difficulty without even the time to give it serious thought. It is, moreover, easier to gain marks at the lower end of the scale than at the upper, and you will never compensate for one poor answer by further polishing two satisfactory answers. Try to leave some time at the end of the examination to re-read your answers and correct any obvious errors. If the worst comes to the worst and you run short of time, don't just keep writing until you are forced to break off in mid-paragraph. It is far better to provide for the examiner a set of notes which indicate the overall direction of your argument.

Good luck — but if you prepare for the examination conscientiously and tackle the paper in a methodical manner, you won't need it!

deceiving Benedick and Beatrice into 'a mountain of affection th'one with th'other' (II.1.339–340). The basis of both plots is getting the victims to overhear other people speaking, as they think, honestly.

In fact, therefore, we are being presented with two types of deceit: that which is benevolent, like Don Pedro's or the Friar's, seeking ultimately a harmony that can be expressed ~~in~~ marriage, and that which is totally destructive, like Don J~~ohn's~~. The success of each type of deceit depends on a manipul~~ation of~~ language and an alteration of behaviour and appearances ~~and~~ on the readiness of the victims to judge from what is pres~~ented to~~ their eyes and ears. Telling the two types apart may ~~be diffic~~ult.

It is not as if any character is unaware of the diffi~~c~~ult ~~relati~~onship of appearance to reality: but nearly every one is led ~~to ch~~oose, of two alternatives, the wrong one. The best instance of this comes at the crisis of the play:

> HERO   ... seemed I ever otherwise to you?
> CLAUDIO   Out of thee! Seeming! I will write against it.
>   You seem to me as Dian in her orb,
>   As chaste as is the bud ere it be blown;
>   But you are more intemperate in your blood
>   Than Venus, or those pampered animals
>   That rage in savage sensuality.

(IV.1.53–59)

Hero's innocent use of the word 'seemed' — not 'was' — gets Claudio on the raw, for it raises the issue of behaviour versus real nature that is the cause of his torment. It triggers ~~his~~ remarkable anticipation of Othello's tortured animal im~~agery~~ that highlights the emotional perception of the disju~~nction~~ between appearance and what Claudio at this point beli~~eves to~~ be reality. He could not be more wrong; and he is wrong ~~because~~ he trusted the suspect word of Don John and what he w~~anted~~ to see at Hero's window rather than the woman he ch~~o~~se to ~~have~~ as his wife. Love must, as both Desdemona (*Othello*) and Cordelia (*King Lear*) know, depend on trust: it (or its lack) can never be *proved*. Claudio is given 'ocular proof' (*Othello* III.3.360) of Hero's apparent unchastity, just as Othello is of Desdemona's by Iago, a stage-managing and manipulating

---

Annotations:

short prose quotation incorporated in the text of the essay, within quotation marks.

long verse quotation indented and introduced by a colon. No quotation marks are needed.

Three dots (ellipsis) indicate where words or phrases have been cut from quotation or where (as here) a quotation begins mid-sentence.

Line reference given directly after the quotation, in brackets.

book/play titles are given in italics. In a handwritten or typed manuscript this would appear as underlining: King Lear; Othello.

Short verse quotation incorporated in the text of the essay within quotation marks. If the quotation ran on into a second line of poetry, this would be indicated by a slash (/).

We have divided the following information into two sections. Part A describes those rules which it is essential to master no matter what kind of essay you are writing (including examination answers). Part B sets out some of the more detailed conventions which govern the documentation of essays.

PART A: LAYOUT

Titles of texts

Titles of published books, plays (of any length), long poems, pamphlets and periodicals (including newspapers and magazines), works of classical literature, and films should be underlined: e.g. David Copperfield (novel), Twelfth Night (play), Paradise Lost (long poem), Critical Quarterly (periodical), Horace's Ars Poetica (Classical work), Apocalypse Now (film).

Notice how important it is to distinguish between titles and other names. Hamlet is the play; Hamlet the prince. Wuthering Heights is the novel; Wuthering Heights the house. Underlining is the equivalent in handwritten or typed manuscripts of printed italics. So what normally appears in this volume as *Othello* would be written as Othello in your essay.

Titles of articles, essays, short stories, short poems, songs, chapters of books, speeches, and newspaper articles are enclosed in quotation marks; e.g. 'The Flea' (short poem), 'The Prussian Officer' (short story), 'Middleton's Chess Strategies' (article), 'Thatcher Defects!' (newspaper headline).

Exceptions: Underlining titles or placing them within quotation marks does not apply to sacred writings (e.g. Bible, Koran, Old Testament, Gospels) or parts of a book (e.g. Preface, Introduction, Appendix).

It is generally incorrect to place quotation marks around a title of a published book which you have underlined. The exception is 'titles within titles': e.g. 'Vanity Fair': A Critical Study (title of a book about *Vanity Fair*).

Quotations

Short verse quotations of a single line or part of a line should be incorporated within quotation marks as part of the running text of your essay. Quotations of two or three lines of verse are treated in the same way, with line endings indicated by a slash(/). For example:

1   In Julius Caesar, Antony says of Brutus, 'This was the noblest Roman of them all'.
2   The opening of Antony's famous funeral oration, 'Friends, Romans, Countrymen, lend me your ears;/ I come to bury Caesar not to praise him', is a carefully controlled piece of rhetoric.

Longer verse quotations of more than three lines should be indented from the main body of the text and introduced in most cases with a colon. Do not enclose indented quotations within quotation marks. For example:

It is worth pausing to consider the reasons Brutus gives to justify his decision to assassinate Caesar:

> It must be by his death; and for my part,
> I know no personal cause to spurn at him,
> But for the general. He would be crowned.
> How might that change his nature, there's the question.

At first glance his rationale may appear logical . . .

Prose quotations of less than three lines should be incorporated in the text of the essay, within quotation marks. Longer prose quotations should be indented and the quotation marks omitted. For example:

1   Before his downfall, Caesar rules with an iron hand. His political opponents, the Tribunes Marullus and Flavius, are 'put to silence' for the trivial offence of 'pulling scarfs off Caesar's image'.
2   It is interesting to note the rhetorical structure of Brutus's Forum speech:

> Romans, countrymen, and lovers, hear me for my cause, and be silent that you may hear. Believe me for my honour, and have respect to mine honour that you may believe. Censure me in your wisdom, and awake your senses, that you may the better judge.

Tenses: When you are relating the events that occur within a work of fiction or describing the author's technique, it is the convention to use the present tense. Even though Orwell published *Animal Farm* in 1945, the book *describes* the animals' seizure of Manor Farm. Similarly, Macbeth always *murders* Duncan, despite the passage of time.

PART B: DOCUMENTATION

When quoting from verse of more than twenty lines, provide line references: e.g. In 'Upon Appleton House' Marvell's mower moves 'With whistling scythe and elbow strong' (1.393).

Quotations from plays should be identified by act, scene and line references: e.g. Prospero, in Shakespeare's The Tempest, refers to Caliban as 'A devil, a born devil' (IV.1.188). (i.e. Act 4. Scene 1. Line 188).

Quotations from prose works should provide a chapter reference and, where appropriate, a page reference.

Bibliographies should list full details of all sources consulted. The way in which they are presented varies, but one standard format is as follows:

1 Books and articles are listed in alphabetical order by the author's last name. Initials are placed after the surname.
2 If you are referring to a chapter or article within a larger work, you list it by reference to the author of the article or chapter, not the editor (although the editor is also named in the reference).
3 Give (in parentheses) the place and date of publication, e.g. (London, 1962). These details can be found within the book itself. Here are some examples:

Brrockbank, J. P., 'Shakespeare's Histories, English and Roman', in Ricks, C. (ed.) English Drama to 1710 (Sphere History of Literature in the English Language) (London, 1971).

Gurr, A., 'Richard III and the Democratic Process', Essays in Criticism 24 (1974), pp. 39–47.

Spivack, B., Shakespeare and the Allegory of Evil (New York, 1958).

Footnotes: In general, try to avoid using footnotes and build your references into the body of the essay wherever possible. When you do use them give the full bibliographic reference to a work in the first instance and then use a short title: e.g. See K. Smidt, <u>Unconformities in Shakespeare's History Plays</u> (London, 1982), pp. 43–47 becomes Smidt (pp. 43–47) thereafter. Do not use terms such as 'ibid.' or 'op. cit.' unless you are absolutely sure of their meaning.

There is a principle behind all this seeming pedantry. The reader ought to be able to find and check your references and quotations as quickly and easily as possible. Give additional information, such as canto or volume number whenever you think it will assist your reader.

SUGGESTIONS FOR FURTHER READING

Texts

Norman Sanders New Penguin edition of *Julius Caesar* (Harmondsworth, 1967) provides a reliable text and stimulating introductory essay. The New Cambridge edition, edited by Marvin Spivack (Cambridge, 1985), provides more detailed annotation and an introductory essay which pays particular attention to the stage history of the play.

Critical studies

Cantor, Paul, *Shakespeare's Rome: Republic and Empire* (Cambridge, 1976)

Leggatt, Alexander, *Shakespeare's Political Drama: The History Plays and the Roman Plays* (London, 1989)

Miola, Robert, *Shakespeare's Rome* (Cambridge, 1983)

Simmons, J, *Shakespeare's Pagan World: The Roman Tragedies* (Virginia, 1988)

Spencer, T J B, *Shakespeare's Plutarch* (Harmondsworth, 1964)

Traversi, D A, *The Roman Plays* (London, 1963)

Ure, Peter, *Julius Caesar: A Casebook* (Basingstoke, 1969)

Wilson, Richard, *Julius Caesar: a Critical Study* (Harmondsworth, 1991)

Longman Group Limited
*Longman House, Burnt Mill, Harlow, Essex, CM20 2JE, England
and Associated Companies throughout the World.*

First published 1992
Second impression 1994
ISBN 0 582 07579 3

*Set in 10/12 pt Century Schoolbook, Linotron 202
Produced by Longman Singapore Publishers (Pte) Ltd
Printed in Singapore*

The Publisher's policy is to use paper manufactured from
sustainable forests.

Acknowledgement
The editors would like to thank Zachary Leader for his assistance with
the style sheet.